Books by Dean Gualco

What Happened to the American Dream (1995)

The Meaning of Life (2005)

The Great People of our Time (2008)

The Good Manager: A Guide to the 21st Century Manager (2010)

The Choices and Consequences of our Age: The Disintegrating Political, Economic, and Societal Institutions of the United States (2012)

Making a Difference: Changing the World in Which You Live (2013)

Words to Live By: Quotes and Stories That Inspire Our Time on Earth (2016)

TAKE
the
RIGHT ROAD

Finding the Right Job,
Being the Right Employee, and
Becoming the Right Person

DEAN GUALCO

TAKE THE RIGHT ROAD
FINDING THE RIGHT JOB, BEING THE RIGHT EMPLOYEE, AND BECOMING THE RIGHT PERSON

iUniverse books may be ordered through booksellers or by contacting:

iUniverse
1663 Liberty Drive
Bloomington, IN 47403
www.iuniverse.com
1-800-Authors (1-800-288-4677)

ISBN: 978-1-5320-6067-0 (sc)
ISBN: 978-1-5320-6069-4 (hc)
ISBN: 978-1-5320-6068-7 (e)

Library of Congress Control Number: 2018912595

Print information available on the last page.

iUniverse rev. date: 10/18/2018

In the midst of unparalleled progress,
a growing sense of insecurity and instability
pervades a generation unable to find a good job,
losing their future to the growing army of robots
that work cheaper and better than humans,
and to the creation of artificial intelligence
that thinks faster and more intelligently
than humans ever could.

It is an ironic twist of fate:
the very technology designed to create a better world
is now on the precipice
of destroying the opportunity for society to achieve it.

To my children, Gunner and Tori,
who have given me a blessed life.

"always look for the good along the road of life"

I have long believed that if you can dream the impossible dream, be determined to achieve it, never fear failure or what other people think, work hard, do what's right, and always look for the good, then you will have greatness within your grasp. Fame and fortune are not the determining factors of a great life but rather that you fought the good fight, did the best you could with what you had, did what is right, and made a difference in some small way. It has been a great ride, and for that I have been blessed, and I am thankful to many who have helped me along my path in life. Some of those people are:

- The Man Upstairs: You have made this all possible.
- To Mom and Dad: Few have ever done more for their children than my parents.
- My maternal grandmother, Vee McCoy, and paternal grandparents, Bocci and Rose Gualco: You gave me a good reputation to live up to.
- Bill Munroe: Friends come and go, but there always seems to be one or two you have for life. Thanks for being one of those friends.
- John and Rachel Ellis: Find a loyal friend like John and Rachel, and you will be set for life. I have been blessed.
- Sierra and Shana Brucia. You are two of the most decent and honorable people I have ever met. When the chips are down, your number is one of the first I call.
- Jeff Thompson: You are a good man who is trying to do good things.
- My sister: Just because.
- Finally, to Jon Smith: I knew Jon from the second grade until my freshman year of college, when he was killed by a drunk driver. He was one of the best guys I've ever met—or will ever meet. He never had the chance to live his life and reach his destiny. Jon died more than thirty years ago, and while his chance to make a difference was short-lived, this fact pushes me to make a difference with whatever time I have been granted on this earth.

This Book

In 2017, my son, Gunner, graduated with an engineering degree from the University of the Pacific, and in 2018, my daughter, Tori, graduated with a liberal arts degree from the University of Arizona. Both received exceptional educations from distinguished universities, yet finding the good job—one that offered a decent start to a promising future—appeared elusive. There are too few opportunities for them to pursue, which is the case for many recent college graduates and nearly anyone else seeking a job in today's world.

More than at any time in recent history, one of the lessons to be learned is that we have to make it on our own. Time may be fleeting, and boulders might impede nearly every road we travel, but for those who work hard, are kind, overcome their challenges, conquer their insecurities, do what is right, and live decent and honorable lives, there are possibilities. We can use our talents, educations, and experiences to do something great with what we have and what we have been given. We may not shape the history that will define our generation, but we can do something. Along the way, we can make a small difference in the world—if we have a guide to do so.

Using my decades of experiences in the management, human resources, and educational field – during which I served as a human resource director for multiple public and private organizations, interviewed and hired thousands of individuals, and managed a career counseling and outreach program for a major university – I have written this book to serve as a guide for my son and daughter and others like them who seek not just to make a living but to make a life and to seek something better along their walk through history. It is my hope that, through the pages of this book, readers will be inspired to not only dream the impossible dream but also to be determined to achieve it. Anything is possible if you are willing to work for it. I learned this lesson from my grandparents and then from my parents.

I have learned many other lessons along the unimaginable roads I have traveled. Some led to victory, others defeat, but no one goes through life unscathed and undefeated. These lessons form the cornerstone of this book and are best summarized in this short poem:

I Have Learned...

As the sands of life fall in the hourglass, I've learned that:

we must work hard and be nice to others;
we can dream the impossible dream but
also be determined to achieve it;
that we have far more power to control our future
than others do to destroy it;
and that it's not what we were given that is important,
but what we do with what we were given that matters.

I've learned that:

no matter the obstacle, regardless of the
challenge, irrespective of the sacrifice,
we must stand for something, work for something,
and fight for something that is decent, honorable, and just ...
all the while never faltering or wavering,
never giving in or giving up,
and never fearing failure or what others think.

I've learned that:

what is right always triumphs over what is wrong,
that kindness always triumphs over hatred,
that goodness always triumphs over evil.

Finally, I've learned that:

what matters is not whether we achieved
our hopes or realized our dreams
what matters is whether we tried ...
tried to *be* good, tried to *do* good,
tried to make *someone* better, tried to make *something* better

that we fought the good fight,
that we did the best we could with what we had,
that we did what was right ... and that, in some small way,
we made a difference

And that brings me to my eternal wish, and hope, for you:
that as you enter the last days of your life
you will be grateful for the gift of time you were granted
and believe you did something good with
the time you were granted
so you can look back ...
on a life that has been lived,
on a life that had purpose,
on a life that mattered.
and on a life that always looked for the
good along the road you traveled.

CONTENTS

We live in a land of unimagined opportunities,
within a world of unlimited possibilities,
at least for those…
who dream the impossible dream,
work hard to achieve it,
are kind to all they meet,
and overcome any obstacle in their path.

INTRODUCTION

Economies shatter, governments fall, societies clash, yet the world evolves. From depressions to earthquakes, diseases to wars, history is replete with cataclysmic events that affect and reshape the fate of generation after generation. Rarely does a century pass without a considerable, even transformational, change to the manner in which we work and the culture in which we live. In the twenty-first century, the most consequential event may be the disruption and turmoil caused by an economy that is unable to provide a good and decent job to a society clamoring for some sense of economic security and social stability.

In times past, when one industry fell, another rose. When one job vanished, another appeared. Advancements in science and technology, the twin factors most responsible in a world's transformation, created new economics that enabled their societies to realize a rising standard of living. Farming evolved into industrialization, industrialization into manufacturing, and manufacturing into services, and in each metamorphosis, people progressed toward something more promising and something better. For some, if not many, that progress has stalled, and the promise of something better remains distant.

Finding the right job may seem elusive, but for those who exhaustively explore opportunities, thoroughly prepare for interviews, extensively build relationships across industries, and never stop looking for a job, the good job can still be found. Being the right employee may appear a remote possibility, but for those who work hard, think differently, adapt, and adjust to changing environments, and are loyal to and care about their organization and its people, a good future can still be found. Finally, becoming the right person may seem daunting, but for those who do the best with what they have, ensure they have options in life, always look for the good along the roads they travel, let others live lives of negativity and misery, are extraordinary kindhearted, and go down swinging for who they are and what they stand for, a good life can still be lived.

In the end, nothing may seem to last, and the journey may be littered with the forsaken dreams and forgotten hopes of the fallen, but for those who are willing to work hard, are kind and generous to all they meet, and overcome any obstacle and triumph through any challenge, greatness will touch their lives.

never abdicate your belief, or abandon your hope,
that you can make something better,
that you can make a difference …

these are the ones destined for greatness
and the consequential few in our world's history.

I

A DIFFERENT WORLD

My father was raised by immigrants from Italy. My grandparents could not afford to travel to the United States from Italy, so my grandfather borrowed money to make the trip, and then he spent several years paying back the money. He and his wife built a farming business, a challenging occupation for someone who could not speak the language and had little family to rely upon. But they persevered, raising three sons in the process. My father, the middle son, worked almost ten hours a day on the family farm while attending school, and then he accepted his first job at sixteen at a garbage company. Several years later, he bought an equal ownership share into the garbage company, borrowing the money to do so from his father, which he paid back over several years.

For thirty years, my father worked and served as a part owner of that garbage company. Located in the Bay Area, he missed only ten days of work during those years (excluding vacations, even counting the birth of his four children), all the while investing his hard-earned salary into the purchase of land, commercial properties, and other investments. He intended to create and build a business that will sustain his and my mother's lives far through retirement and then provide a future for their children and grandchildren.

My mother had a more challenging background. She was raised in a single-parent household. Her father left his wife, my grandmother, for another woman when my mother was four years old. My grandfather never paid any child support, forcing my mother and her sister to rely upon welfare for their food and clothing. There were few opportunities for my grandmother to work outside the home at that time, so she supplemented her income through sewing and babysitting. It was an extremely difficult childhood.

At eighteen, my mother started her first job, and she worked continually for the next sixty years, long after her children and grandchildren graduated from college. Though long past the financial need to work, my mother still devoted part of her time and a significant amount of her money to help those who may not have been as fortunate as she has been. Work is all my parents have known.

My parents were born into a generation where you worked hard, created your own financial stability and future, saved for the inevitable rainy day, and gave something back to your community. It really was a simple life with simple values. You make something of the life in which you were born, no matter who you were born to, where you were born, where you were raised, or the circumstances in which you lived. It was a simpler time with simple values, but those values were shared by a generation. Working, saving, and helping your fellow citizens permeated throughout the society of the day.

Over the past century, the world has changed, in many ways good and others not good. Today, women and minorities are treated more fairly and more equally than at any time in our nation's history. This is, without reservation or doubt, the most significant political and social change over the past several centuries. Our educational system is more progressive, allowing those with learning disabilities and language barriers to receive better educations. Research and discoveries have revolutionized the medical field, eradicating many diseases and developing surgical procedures and medicines that have extended the lives of even the sickest and most injured people. Finally, advances in technology and communication have created products and services—from Apple to Facebook to Tesla—that have remade and reshaped the world in which we live. Even the most foresighted individual in the 1950s or even 1980s could not have imagined this world.

However, even the most advanced countries such as the United States, Germany, Great Britain, and Norway, are challenged to sustain a standard of living for their citizens equal to one created ten or twenty years ago. In the 1950s and 1960s, American citizens were enjoying a constantly rising standard of living. Economic opportunities were plentiful, accompanied by ever-increasing wages and benefits, and workers enjoyed company-paid retirement and health care and guaranteed or lifetime employment. It was common for an individual to work thirty or thirty-five years at the same company, as my father did, and then live the remainder of their lives on a retirement paid for by the company. Economically and politically, the United States was at its zenith. At one point, it was producing almost 40 percent of all goods and services in the world while possessing only 6 percent of the world's population.

It was the age of the American, but history presages that few ages last. The dominant country of today is often the fallen country of tomorrow. By the 1970s, after decades of dominance, the United States began its slide. Though still the dominant political and military country on the globe, its economic growth slowed, principally because those countries decimated by World War II had rebuilt and retooled their industries to compete against the United States. These countries had lower wages, lower taxes, and lower government regulations. By the 1970s, they were producing and selling their goods to the United States at a lower cost.

The higher wages and benefits of the typical American worker during this time had raised the prices of American goods and services beyond what could be purchased from other countries. Lower-cost foreign products—coupled with the stunning advances in computers, technology, and telecommunication—fundamentally altered the economic and societal underpinning of a once-stable country. In the United States, jobs were no longer plentiful, and those that were available were increasingly geared toward the skilled and knowledgeable, dividing a society into the haves and have-nots, and promoting political and societal challenges the country has still not yet addressed or resolved in any substantive and meaningful way.

A Different Country

For too many, regret and sadness consume their past;
for too few, hope and happiness inspire their future.

For the United States, the latter half of the twentieth century has been a period of great achievements and great disappointments.

Economically, the United States dominated the world's economy, yet not all Americans have benefited from those heady times. Politically, the populace lost confidence in its elected leaders as one scandal after another—from Watergate to Iran-Contra, and Monica Lewinsky to the Iraq War—has eroded the basic public trust necessary to govern a country, resulting in a slew of less-experienced political candidates running for the office of president, from Jimmy Carter to Bill Clinton, George W. Bush to Donald Trump. And socially, the divisiveness that represented the 1960s continues unabated into the twenty-first century, as the rich battle the poor, the educated against less educated, the old versus the young, men against women, Democrats facing the Republications, management opposed by unions, and one person's history across from another. It is far from the ideals espoused by this country's founders of a freer country, a fairer country, and a more favorable country.

For too many, we live in a fragmented land defined by what separates and divides rather than by what connects and unites. Jealously, envy, and hate seem to dominate the emotions of those who have little against those who have much, no matter the effort or sacrifice expended to attain what someone may have. Those on both ends of the political spectrum seem incapable of listening to or appreciating a different viewpoint, and it seems more are critical of the differences among our citizenry rather than accepting a uniqueness that makes our country an interesting realm to live and travel. The shining light of attaining something better seems to have been extinguished for many in the United States, a circumstance foreign to those who built a country that once represented the ideals of hope and dreams, both of which rescued the world from two world wars and an economic depression in the twentieth century.

These same hopes and dreams seem powerless and incapable of rescuing the United States from its greatest challenge since the Civil War, the Great Depression, and World War I and II: the inability of the average American to find and maintain a good job that offers the safety of continued employment and the security of medical and retirement benefits to provide for their continued health and financial status. These losses have—more than any other factor since World War II—affected the economic, political, and societal country in which we live. The economy cannot produce enough jobs for its citizens, causing a hallowing out of the middle classes and a rise in homelessness, income inequality, crime, poverty, and debt. The political subdivisions cannot generate enough revenues to support the generous social benefits their voters demand, resulting in a lack of faith and trust in their leadership. Finally, society has been rocked by a competition for diminishing financial resources, pitting individuals against individuals, groups against groups, in an effort to obtain a larger or similar slice of the same or diminishing pie.

It has become the challenge of our age: to maintain a stable political and societal system while the economic system crumbles, a system that has proven unable to produce a sufficient number of jobs to supports its citizenry. With an exploding political system requiring an increasingly higher amount of monies to support its social programs—and a society that is increasingly unable to adequately maintain its current standard of living— myriad stresses have combined to wreak havoc on a country struggling to meet its obligations to its people and their future.

A Different Economy

The United States, as most would surmise, is a much different country than it was upon its founding in 1776. The country was created through a political philosophy that espoused limited government, low taxes, nonexistent regulations, near-unlimited immigration, and the requirement that its citizens "make it on their own." There were few social programs for the disadvantaged and disabled, and they turned to families, churches, and charities for assistance. This was the time of the "rugged individual" of the American frontier who would seize the day, creating their own future and living with the consequences of their subsequent success and failure.

As much as economically and politically, society has profoundly changed since our nation's founding more than two centuries ago. Women and minorities are assuming their rightful place in society, and by utilizing their ambitions and talents, the country has progressed far beyond those countries who stifle or suppress a certain segment of their society. The countries that suppress the intellectual capabilities, talents, and spirits of their citizens rarely achieve their grand ambitions. Those citizens who are not allowed, or are incapable of, becoming functioning and contributing members of society must be supported by others, a circumstance that diverts precious energies and monies from more productive pursuits to others who are held back from achieving their potential because of outdated or outmoded beliefs. Most countries have banished these biases and prejudices, creating more diverse and inclusive countries that politically support and societally encourage their citizens to pursue interests that benefit the entirety of the country.

While our forefathers would not have recognized the society of today, they would hardly have recognized the economy of today either. Agriculture dominated the economy in the late eighteenth century; by the nineteenth century, manufacturing had replaced agriculture. Technology (including the use of pesticides, better farming practices, and machinery) allowed food production to increase exponentially while utilizing fewer acres of land. This same technology created the manufacturing sector, moving thousands from the farms to the cities to work in manufacturing plants. Technology, likewise, changed the face of manufacturing. The use of machines reduced the need for a great number of workers to produce an equal number of products.

That, too, was not long to last. By the twentieth century, manufacturing gave way to the service sector. Science and technology have allowed the world to create more products with fewer employees, and transportation has allowed companies to ship these products throughout the globe in a cost-effective manner. The world has turned, instead, to using employees to provide services. Rather than making an actual product, the United States economy is now driven by services such as retail, education, health care, and computers. In 2017, services created and performed in the United States account for about 66 percent of the nation's total economic activity (Mutikani, 2017), a figure similar to the world's percent of total economic activity produced by services, which is 69 percent (Statista, 2018).

Through we have many more products through science and technology, we also have fewer employment opportunities within manufacturing, displacing millions of people from the workforce. They have transitioned to services, but we are soon to see many more millions of service sector jobs being replaced the upcoming onslaught of robots and artificial intelligence.

A Different Industry

Accept your fate—or have the will to change it.

When the United States was founded, about 90 percent of the four million people who called this country their home made their living through agriculture (Cummins, 2018). It was the era of the "rugged" American, so named because many of these farmers managed their own land and ran their own small businesses, and it was hard, time-consuming work where families relied on almost no one other than themselves to make their living. This was a time with virtually no mechanized equipment, and fields had to be planted, tilled, and harvested by hand. From sunup to sundown, the work never seemed to cease, and adverse weather or illness could devastate a family and its community. It was a backbreaking existence with little opportunity for family members to do anything else but support the family enterprise, mainly because science, technology, communications, and transportation had not advanced to create the market for industries and professions that would allow farmers to move away from their lands.

Soon, these factors changed. Power was once the domain of man and the horse; by the early 1800s, science and technology were able to harness power on an unprecedented scale. Starting with the steam engine and continuing with the internal-combustion engine and electricity, the scale of innovations was beyond comprehension. In a manner of fifty years, industrial and manufacturing complexes were created—utilizing these new advances in power—to create and build products that soon served the masses. Concurrently, advances in farming machinery and techniques meant fewer family members were needed to produce agricultural crops, causing a surplus of labor in the agrarian industry. While more than 90 percent the United States working population worked in agriculture in the late 1700s, by the 1850s, only 64 percent of the working population, or 7.7 million people, worked in agriculture (*New York Times*, 1988). It was a perfect storm. As the need for employees to work in the nation's largest employment sector (farming) fell, the need for employees to work in industry and manufacturing exploded; thus began the great migration of people from farming to manufacturing.

At the time, the 1800s were seen as the watershed time of global progress. Countries harnessed the imagination and ingenuity of their citizens to build massive factories and produce goods and services on an unprecedented scale. Never before had so much been manufactured to serve so many, from textiles to telephones, steam engines to steamboats, cameras to canals, and railroads to refrigerators. Brilliant inventors of that time became famous for all time, from Samuel Morse (telegraph) to Isaac Singer (sewing machine), Charles Goodyear (rubber) to George Westinghouse (transistor and air brake), shaping a world where many were able to share in this virtually endless bounty of products (Kelly, 2018). It may also have been the first time in history that so many benefited from the growth in technology, helping form a middle class that built these new products and could afford to purchase them. If the 1800s were a period of historic change, few could have predicted that the late twentieth century would bring a level of growth and change unforeseen and unimagined in human history.

By the twentieth century, the world looked and acted much different. An era of scientific exploration and advancement permeated most of industry and society, creating new industries to work in and new lands to live in. The United States invented—or led the world in conceiving—the automobile and the airplane, radios and rockets, motion pictures and magnetic tapes, television and the internet. The country eradicated polio and found ways to control measles, mumps, rubella, smallpox, diphtheria, tuberculosis, and malaria, diseases that caused the deaths of millions in centuries past. Dams were constructed, bridges and skyscrapers were built, the personal computer was invented, and men traveled to the moon. Nothing, it seemed, became beyond the capability of the engineer or scientist, architect or inventor, except for the ability to predict where most of America's workers were going to find the next industry to work in and the next job to apply for.

A Different Job

If you aren't preparing for the next job,
you're preparing to lose your current job.

There are three general economic sectors of an economy: the primary sector (involving raw materials, which center around agriculture, mining, and fishing), the secondary sector (chiefly finished goods produced by factories and manufacturing plants), and the service sector (which are intangible goods and services). As a country develops, its economy moves from a primary economy to one based on the service sector (Pegginger, 2017), mainly because there are greater revenues and profits to be gained through the service economy. Doctors and lawyers, more often, make more than laborers and farmers. The economic growth of the United States, since its founding, followed this trend. The percentage of Americans working on farms has fallen to its lowest percentage in history, just 1.4 percent of total American employees works on a farm (Ag and Food Sectors of the Economy, 2018). From the primary sector, the United States evolved into the secondary sector, aided by the innovations of science and technology (the United States now dominates the service sector throughout the world).

From the nineteenth through the early twentieth century, there was a dramatic increase in the percentage of Americans working in manufacturing. However, by the later twentieth century, the percentage of Americans working in manufacturing—designing and building products sold throughout the world—had fallen dramatically. In the 1970s, 26 percent of Americans were employed in manufacturing, but by 2017, just 10 percent of United States workers were employed in manufacturing (Buttonwood, 2017). Manufacturing jobs are becoming increasingly the domain of foreign countries—not only in terms of location or frequency but also of opportunity. Most Americans now work in the service sector, an area of the economy where employees do not necessarily produce a product but rather a service such as working in retail stores, education, financial, health care, and computer services.

The United States does not make much anymore, and with that fall has been a dramatic loss in the stable and profitable employment offered to employees in the manufacturing sector. In 1990, there were thirty-six states where more people worked in manufacturing than any other industry; by 2014, there were only seven states where most of the state's working population worked in manufacturing (Wilson, 2014). During that period alone, six million people lost their jobs in the manufacturing sector, and many accepted jobs in the service sector. By 2014, health care and social assistance industries were the dominant employers in thirty-four states; retail employers were the dominant source of jobs in another ten states. Compounding the loss of manufacturing jobs is that service sector jobs generally pay less than manufacturing jobs. Workers in manufacturing generally make 9 percent more than workers in other industries, and the difference is especially pronounced for those without a college degree working in manufacturing. Those without a four-year college degree working in the manufacturing sector still make about $150 more per week than those in other industries (Wilson, 2014; Stettner, Yudken, and McCormack, 2017).

Part of the shift from manufacturing to the service sector is related to the economic condition of producing a product (or working) in the United States, which demands higher corporate taxes and broader business regulations than some other countries. However, the most significant factor related to the loss of jobs in manufacturing is related to technology and productivity. A recent Ball State University study concluded that the vast majority of lost jobs—88 percent—were merely because we no longer need humans to manufacture products (Wiseman, 2016).

Robots now do the jobs of employees—and at a much lower cost. As an example, General Motors employs less than one-third of the 600,000 workers it had in the 1970s, but the company still produces more cars and trucks. In another example, from 1997 to 2016, American production of steel increased 18 percent, but with 42 percent fewer workers, A total of 265,000 fewer people now work in the steel industry (Wiseman, 2016). Add in the high cost of doing business in the United States, from rising employee salary and benefit costs, high taxes and regulations, and exorbitant costs related to land acquisition and construction of plants and equipment, it becomes apparent that entrepreneurs and their organizations must search for other opportunities to achieve growth and productivity instead of hiring additional employees.

In numerous industries, robots have become the "employee" of choice because they are more productive, have fewer errors, are easier to buy (or hire) and dispose of (or terminate employment), cannot sue their employers, do not get injured on the job, do not get sick, do not mandate an array of ever-increasing benefits (social security, unemployment or disability insurance), and do not require additional employees to meet their needs (payroll, human resources, risk managers, attorneys, etc.).

From mechanical arms to building automobiles, from robot-assisted medical procedures to intricate surgeries, from filling prescriptions to automated tellers and clerks, the technology we created to make our lives easier has now eased many out of a job, a profession, or even a future. And, importantly, robots are becoming even cheaper to buy and use. Robots are not isolated to the domain of the largest and best-funded corporations as more mid-to-small firms can now have access to, and afford, robots and robotics. As an example, Boston Consulting recently reported that a robotic spot welder now costs $133,000 a year to buy and operate, down from $182,000 in 2005, and it is projected to fall further to $103,000 by 2025 (AP, 2016).

The search for lower production and employee costs, and greater efficiency, means that robots and artificial intelligence will become the dominating factor in the development and production of nearly anything we buy and sell in the coming decades. By the early 2030s, it is estimated that nearly 38 percent of all US jobs will be at high risk of being automated—and few industries are expected to offer humans a replacement job (Masunaga, 2017). Between 2017 and 2027 alone, robots are expected to create more than 15 million jobs in the United States, a figure that amounts to about 10 percent of our national workforce (Catey, 2017). What is becoming true is that the human workforce is being replaced by the inhuman workforce.

Whereas efficiencies in farming led employees to seek and secure employment in manufacturing, and efficiencies in manufacturing led employees to seek and secure employment in services, today technologies have led manufacturing and services industries to seek and secure employment for robots, rather than humans, to meet their needs in a more economical and efficient manner. Here is a startling statistic: McKinsey Global Institute states that as a result of artificial intelligence, about one-third of all United States workers will need to find another job within the next twelve years (Williams, 2017). And, nearly no industries are not immune to the onslaught of work performed by robots and artificial intelligence. Here are some of the more prominent advances projected in robotic (as opposed to human) employment:

- American factories now make 85 percent more than they did in 1987 with two-thirds fewer workers (Manjoo, 2017). Technology and computerization have decimated this employment sector.
- Robots are expected to perform about 25 percent of all manufacturing tasks by 2025, up from 10 percent today (Sirkin, Zinser, and Rose, 2015).
- For every industrial robot used in the workplace, six human jobs are eliminated (Glaser and Molla, 2017).
- Apple and Samsung replaced more than 60,000 employees with robots in 2016, and one major manufacturer is now replacing 90 percent of its workers with robots (MSN, 2016).
- Automation has cut the number of people working at the average McDonald's by half since the 1960s (McFarland, 2017).
- Amazon uses more than 45,000 robots in its fulfillment centers to process and fill orders (Catey, 2017).
- At a University of California San Francisco pharmacy, one robot filled more than 350,000 doses of medication during its first month of use. Filling both oral and injectable medicines, even toxic chemotherapy drugs, the robot committed no errors (UCSF News Center, 2011).
- "Robo-surgeons" have performed more than 2 million medical procedures since 2000 (MSN, 2016).
- Uber announced that between 2019 and 2021, they intend to buy 24,000 Volvo automobiles to serve as driverless cars (Williams, 2017).
- By 2030, it is estimated that robots will replace one-fourth of United States combat soldiers serving in the military (Catey, 2017).

Even some jobs considered "safe" by nearly any current or prospective employee are in danger of being replaced by robots and artificial intelligence. There is computer software that reads scans more efficiently than a radiologist, robots that outperform surgeons in certain tests, computers that scan legal papers faster than an attorney, and software that can author newspaper articles about Wall Street earnings and sports (Williams, 2017). The trend is unmistakably, and unfortunately, clear: tasks still need to be accomplished in the workplace, but those tasks are increasingly being taken by computers and technology. As a result, there will be fewer jobs in the coming decades, especially jobs that pay a good wage with solid benefits, and for those jobs that do exist, it will be more competitive for its job seekers to attain.

Summary

Once the American worker looked forward, with great optimism, toward a better paying job, with expanding benefits, and with a promising future of continued employment and promotional opportunities to meet their rising aspirations. While these opportunities may not have always offered the chance to attain a sense of meaning in one's life, they allowed one to provide a good standard of living for a person and their family and allowed them to be a participating member of society. Such are the memories of yesteryear.

Today, an array of statistics attests to the diminishing prospects confronting those in the job market. As of 2015, only about 62 percent of people in the United States actively participate in the labor market (are employed), a fall from 66.4 percent in 1995, and now the lowest level since the 1970s (Federal Reserve Bank of St. Louis, 2017). More sobering is the type of jobs offered to those currently in the workplace: about 40 percent of the US workforce can be classified as "contingent" workers, typically those who are contractors or contract workers, often without a regular income, good benefits, or some guarantee of continued employment. This is an increase from 30 percent in 2005 (Forbes, 2015). In fact, about 90 percent of jobs created from 2005 to 2015 were "contingent" jobs (Durden, 2016), one reason that about 50 percent of all jobs pay less than $18 an hour, or $37,000 a year (Long, 2017), hardly an income that can support an individual let alone a family.

Almost 18 percent of US employees now work part-time, an increase from 13.5 percent in 1968 (Mislinski, 2018). There are 5.6

million part-time workers who would rather work full-time, a 25 percent increase from 4.5 million in 2007, yet full-time opportunities do not exist (MarketWatch, 2017). Fewer full-time jobs and more part-time jobs have resulted in greater struggles for those in the workplace. These figures result in the fact that almost 80 percent of workers now live paycheck to paycheck, 25 percent of workers cannot make ends meet at the end of each month, and 18 percent of workers reduced their retirement contributions in 2016 (Career Builder, 2017). Not surprisingly, in an effort to make ends meet, nearly 30 percent of full-time workers now have a second job (NPR, 2018).

Every generation confronts the challenge of finding the good job, but absent the Great Depression, the current generation may face a more difficult challenge. The next wave of jobs is not being created for workers but for robots and other technologies that use artificial intelligence. The task for those seeking a good or better job may be daunting, but there are jobs to be found by the most knowledgeable, the most skilled, the most diligent, and those who work the hardest to make the most of the opportunities they have.

You can dream of the unattainable
you can hope for the improbable,
but you must do the possible.

2

FINDING THE RIGHT JOB

A good job pays a decent wage, has fair benefits, and offers an opportunity for employees to obtain some material and psychological rewards from their efforts. To some, a good job no longer exists or has faded into oblivion, and recent studies indicate this may be true. Smabaugh, Nunn, Liu, and Nantz (2017) indicate that, after adjusting for inflation, average wages have risen just 10 percent from 1973 to 2017, making the decent wage more uncommon. Doyle (2018) states that employee job tenure is surprisingly short, with the median tenure of employees in their current position at 4.2 years as of 2016, down from 4.6 years in 2014, an indication that workers are moving from job to job at an increasingly higher rate. Finally, in a recent study published by *Forbes*, Sturt and Nordstrom found that only 52.3 percent of workers stated they were satisfied with their job, a considerable decrease from 61.6 percent of those surveyed in 1987 (Sturt and Nordstrom, 2016). The good job, with its decent wages and benefits, along with material and psychological rewards, may have indeed be a relic of a bygone era.

While the good job may be unattainable for many, it can still be obtained by those who possess the traits and characteristics prized by today's organization and follow a coordinated, systematic, and diligent process to find the good job—the right job—in the foreseeable future. The process to find a job is markedly different than in times previous, a circumstance reflective of the globally competitive, technology-laden, multicultural, and fiscally constrained environment in which we live. Other factors complicate the search process, including the state of the economy and the quantify of jobs in a job seeker's preferred location, along with personal factors such as the credentials of the job seeker and the amount of time one devotes to finding a job (Doyle, 2018). Consequently, finding a job today, and into the near future, is an unbelievably complex, multifaceted, and arduous process. It requires time, effort, money, and a positive attitude, all of which do not cease once we find a job. Almost immediately after finding a good job, one must search for the next job because one never knows how long the current position, in the current industry, will last.

Certainly the best prepared, and best positioned, to succeed in any job market are those who have acquired broad knowledges and expansive skills. However, they have also created a systematic and comprehensive process that identifies the right job to pursue and ensures their combination of knowledges and skills are perfectly suited for that job, leaving no doubt or question that they are the most suitable person for that position.

How does one find the right job, and how does one become the right person for that right job? The former question is the focus of this chapter, and the latter is the focus of the next chapter. The process of finding the right job concentrates on four specific strategies:

- explore possibilities
- prepare for the inevitable
- build relationships (networking)
- never stop looking for a job

Exploring the Possibilities

Not all roads lead to a promised land,
but they do offer the promise of something better.

Decisions, actions, recommendations, strategies, and opinions are more sound if determined through research and exploration. Often the most tedious, boring, and neglected aspect of one's personal and professional life, research identifies the wrong road that has been traveled, the neglected road that should have been considered, and the right road that must be traveled. Not all roads traveled lead to a promised land, but those roads that have been determined through committed inquiry, debate, and decision—hallmarks of nearly any research and exploration process—offer the best chance of achieving your desired ends, which is to find the right job.

Research and exploration—in this case, the studious and continuous inquiry to obtain the relevant facts and statistics of current and future employment trends—is a frustrating, time-consuming, and never-ending process. Facts and statistics change, and trends morph over time, but in the current environment, those facts and trends change at an alarmingly high rate that some cannot comprehend—and fewer can anticipate. Yet those who are best prepared for uncertain times are those who spend their efforts trying to best predict where that future may be, and then adjust and align themselves to take advantage of those opportunities. It is not easy, and it may not be enjoyable, but these are the times and circumstances in which we live.

How does one best research and explore job opportunities, or even the right job, for the future? Obtaining this information is significantly less burdensome than in the past, mainly because the information is more readily available. The internet contains a plethora of studies, commentaries, experiments, guidebooks, opinions, and predictions on nearly any aspect of employment, from industry trends to world consumer demand, from organizational structures to organizational opportunities, from job salaries to job requirements, and from job satisfaction to work-life balance. All this information is accessible to those with the time, patience, and diligence to search through hundreds of websites, read thousands of articles, and listen to endless hours of videos. From this information, the future of an industry, profession, or job can be illuminated and even predicted, allowing those seeking to enter that industry, profession, or job to better prepare themselves for the prospect. Knowledges can be obtained, skills can be acquired, and abilities can be developed for an industry, profession, or job that will demand it from its future participants, and those aware of this future and its expectations will be more poised to profit from it … at least for a brief period of time.

It is an uncertain world. Breakthroughs in science have become so profound, and advances in technology so rapid, that the "latest and greatest" product that is designed today is often outdated before it is manufactured and sold. The same is becoming true of an employee's knowledge and skills. The knowledge, skills, capabilities, and abilities that result in obtaining the good job today appear to be insufficient for obtaining the right job tomorrow.

The applicants who are successful in today's job market are those who continually assess the trends of the future and adapt to the realities of new markets. The ability to assess and adapt to a different future is a key strategy for realizing some sense of security in an insecure world. That comes from research and exploration, and those who follow this path have the best chance of achieving their potential and doing so against a crowded marketplace of individuals seeking a diminishing pool of good jobs.

Preparing for the Inevitable

The inevitable inevitably happens.

The second strategy for finding the good job, the right job, is to prepare for the inevitable. There are few uncertainties in the times in which we live, but one certainty is that most employees will now have more jobs in their working lives, and each job will be for a more limited amount of time. The consequence of this unfortunate circumstance is the rising sense of uncertainty and insecurity that has become all too common for a generation seeking a good job. We have learned that, in 2016, the average employee has been in their current job for only 4.2 years (down from 4.6 years only two years earlier), and that by the time the average employee reaches forty years old, they will have between twelve and fifteen different jobs (Doyle, 2018). Job security and stability are elusive characteristics of those in the job market today, and the reasons go far beyond the use of robots, computers, and artificial intelligence.

Employees simply cost too much to employ today, from the rising minimum wage to the exploding cost of required benefits such as social security, unemployment insurance, workers compensation, Medicare, family and medical leave, and health insurance (for those companies with fifty or more full-time employees). To be competitive and attract the best employees, some organizations also offer other, non-required benefits such as dental and vision insurance, sick and vacation leave, and retirement. According to the Bureau of Labor Statistics in 2017, the average cost of employee benefits is $11.31 per hour. The average American employee makes $24.33 per hour (Gartenstein, 2018), meaning that benefit costs now add approximately 50 percent more to the cost to those an organization employs. None of these costs are required or associated with hiring a robot or using a computer.

There are also other non-wage costs associated with hiring employees, all of which have made hiring employees problematic and even disadvantageous. Employee liability and corporate litigation expenses have soared. According to the United States Courts, civil cases (those involving disputes between individuals or corporations) filed in federal court rose 6 percent from 2015 to 2016, reaching a total of 292,076 cases filed (United States Courts, 2017), while total civil cases in state courts remain at about 15 million filings per year (Court Statistic Project, 2017). Total litigation costs for the Fortune 500 are now above $200 billion, or almost 2 percent of their total revenue, costs that could have been allocated to employee hiring and development. Many of these costs are eliminated through the purchase of a robot or the use of artificial intelligence, alternatives to an employer that may damage an applicant or employee's prospect of initial or continued employment.

How challenging has it become to land a job in today's market? One study found that an average of 250 resumes are received for each corporate job opening, with 75 percent automatically denied by an applicant-tracking computer system. Only about five applicants from 250 applications will be called for an interview, and one may receive a job offer (Economy, 2017; Zipjob, 2017). Given these challenges, the triumphant are those who are best prepared for job opportunities before they arise, best equipped to apply and interview against other competent applicants, and best organized to find another job no matter the current position they hold or the diminished prospects that may exist. Those best prepared have a combination of a well-developed history of accomplishments coupled with a laser focus to succeed no matter the competition or odds of eventual success.

The more successful job applicants have created and are determined to follow a comprehensive process that ensures their efforts and resources are directed toward a specific aim and ambition.

This process includes applying for the right job, creating a targeted cover letter, crafting an intriguing resume, and performing in the interview. Each are presented in greater detail below.

Applying for the Right Job

Given the ease in applying for open positions in the market today—often consuming a few minutes to complete an application—applicants have formed the habit of applying for dozens of jobs per week, at times regardless of the requirements of the job or the qualifications an applicant may have to meet, or not meet, those requirements. This approach, called "spray and pray" by human resource professionals, is populated by applicants *spraying* their application materials to almost any job advertisement they find, and then *pray*ing that a human resource professional will find some merit in the application materials and contact the individual for an interview. This practice, however, can be destructive to an applicant's future prospects. Workopolis (2016) found that some employers are so turned off by such obviously unqualified applications that 43 percent of these employers surveyed have blocked these applicants from applying for further positions at their organization in the future. It is a waste of an applicant's time—and for the organization that must process the applications.

What is the right number of jobs to apply for each week? There is not a "best" number, but the appropriate number is to apply for jobs where an applicant meets the minimum qualifications for the job, the essential duties of the position are of interest, and an applicant believes they can make a difference in that position for the organization and for their future. This also assumes the job meets an applicant's salary and location requirements, and the organization and industry are ones they admire. Of course, it also assumes a particular industry is projected to continue offering solid employment opportunities for those seeking to join its ranks.

As mentioned, the more successful job applicants follow a regimented plan to find potential employment, and this plan includes setting certain goals. One can rarely be successful in the job market without applying for a position, so a foremost goal in the process includes applying for a certain number of jobs each day or week. At an absolute minimum, job seekers should apply for at least one position each week to ensure they remain engaged in the market and are aware of certain trends in the industry or market. A more ambitious goal is to apply for a position every two to three days. When in doubt about whether they meet the general requirements—or if they are uncertain if the position is within their specific ambitions—they should apply and make a final determination following the interview process and if they are offered the position (if they become so fortunate). In any case, applicants should apply for positions where a cursory determination concludes that they meet the expectations, it aligns with their ambitions within the industry, and it is a position they see themselves performing for the foreseeable future.

Once the right jobs have been applied for, applicants should ensure they present the right "picture" to an organization, one that best presents a qualified and motivated candidate for the job. The applicant must clearly stand out as *the* candidate the organization should interview for the position. This process begins with crafting a witty, informative, and targeted cover letter along with an intriguing resume.

Creating a Targeted Cover Letter

There is considerable debate on the value of a cover letter. There are those who believe few human resource professionals read cover letters, and there are others who believe that cover letters detract from the central message of a resume. However, well-written cover letters that present the specific skills and knowledge a candidate possesses, along with their past successes in similar positions, can greatly enhance an applicant's chances of obtaining an interview. This can occur only if the cover letter is targeted to a specific job; a generic or blanket cover letter used for each and every position should rarely be utilized. Instead, a cover letter must be tailored to each position, each organization, and each industry, which requires considerable time and commitment.

A well-developed cover letter should address four issues:

1. It must clearly state why an applicant has chosen to apply for this specific position.

2. It must clearly state why the applicant is uniquely and singularly qualified to apply for the position.
3. It must clearly state the successes the applicant has experienced in similar positions.
4. It must clearly state how the organization will benefit from hiring this applicant at this time.

A cover letter should be limited to supporting these criteria without unnecessary elaboration or distracting data and statements. Thus, cover letters should be short (rarely, if ever, longer than one page and more often three to four paragraphs), targeted to a specific message or highlighting a specific skill or accomplishment, and conveying the worth and value an applicant can bring to the organization that chooses to utilize their services.

It is important to remember that cover letters are only one component of an applicant's comprehensive strategy to obtain an interview (the sole focus of a cover letter and resume remains to garner an interview for its subject). Building relationships with those in your intended industry (also known as networking) and crafting an intriguing and differentiating resume are also part of that strategy. That said, the cover letter offers a unique opportunity to convey a subject's qualification to a prospective employer in a more personal, enthusiastic, and persuasive manner. Applicants should take the time and this opportunity, and make an effort, to restate their qualifications for the position in a cover letter that leaves no doubt that this person is "what the organization is looking for" and explain why the applicant is the person "they are seeking."

One other point that reinforces the importance and value of a well-crafted and well-targeted cover letter: at least historically, resumes tend to be more formal, even mechanical, documents, whereas a cover letter offers an applicant the chance to use more artistic words and creative phrases that speak to the applicant's professional aspirations in a manner that is more personal and more emotional. It is an opportunity for a person (the applicant) to convey their dreams and aspirations to another person (the organization's human resources manager or hiring supervisor) in a manner that touches their heart and soul, hopefully leading those individuals reading the cover letter to state, "This is someone we *have* to meet."

How is that done? In conveying why you are interested, why you are qualified, and why you are the best candidate, the writer should rely on interest, energy, and enthusiasm. An applicant's excitement for the position should jump from the page of a cover letter, while relating how the organization would benefit from the talents and skills of the applicant. The cover letter, as a more personal document, conveys this information in a more conversational tone and manner that "humanizes" the candidate. It is often the first opportunity for an organization to learn who a candidate truly is—and for the candidate to initiate a positive connection with the organization. This is done through utilizing impactful words, powerful phrases, and moving stories that are emotive and professional.

Of course, no matter how well composed and crafted a cover letter is written, it must be read, which often means it must be delivered to the right person. That can be a challenge, which is one reason why cover letters often start "To Whom It May Concern" or "Dear Sir or Madam." However, such salutations often betray the promise of a cover letter, which is to humanize the candidate and excite the organization. Therefore, every effort should be expended to determine who the cover letter and resume should be directed toward. In some cases, that means sending the cover letter and resume to the organization, and also sending direct and personal copies to specific human resources personnel (including the administrative assistant), the hiring department, and those in leadership positions with the organization. This can greatly enhance your opportunity to progress through the recruitment and selection process, and it reinforces the drive and determination that a particular candidate may bring to the position. It may also differentiate a candidate from others, a strategy that may be enough to separate one candidate from another.

In summary, drafting a short, personal, and targeted cover letter enables the organization to see who you are, where you want to go, and where you can take the organization along that journey. It is another opportunity for the organization to know who you are, at least in the written format. In doing so, you can enhance your chances of obtaining an interview, which remains the stated intention of composing and delivering a well-written cover letter (and a resume) to prospective employers.

The choices we make determine our destiny,
and the destiny we pursue determines our legacy.

Crafting an Intriguing Resume

The resume, along with the cover letter, are two important documents that—if written in the right format and tone and delivered to the right employee in an organization—should compel the reader of those documents to state, "I have to meet this person." The resume should intrigue the reader, pique an interest in who the candidate is, and demonstrate how they will help the organization succeed.

The resume is the most critical document to compose and provide to prospective employers in the recruitment process. The candidate must produce and present a phenomenal document that is a written statement—a historical record—of their work history. It should state what they have done and the advances and achievements that they have been largely responsible for (rarely does anyone attain great heights of success through their sole efforts). The resume should state what an applicant's future ambitions are (often relayed in the "career focus" or "career objective" section of the resume) along with how this position is consistent and is an extension of that ambition. Education and experiences form a central role in a resume, which present their background (e.g., colleges attended and organizations employed) along with what they did that was meritorious (e.g., a 4.0 grade point average, increased sales 34 percent over a two-year period). Finally, a section on civil and community contributions offers the candidate an opportunity to present a more well-rounded candidate to an employer, one committed to helping others and serving their community, traits that may raise the profile of an organization in the community and attract new customers.

One of the central ambitions of a resume is, through a series of statistics and statements, making a direct link between what a person has accomplished in the past and how those accomplishments will benefit the organization that employs the candidate in the future. The resume should convey to a recruiter, human resource professional, or organization what they can expect if the applicant joins their team, based mainly from what they have done on the previous teams they were a part of. Here is a simplistic example: if a baseball player batted .305 in the previous four years, the expectations is that they will do so again no matter what team they join. The same should be true of an applicant and an employee: if a new director reorganized, renovated, and revitalized a city's library during their employment, other libraries should expect a similar level of achievement if they hired this applicant, and a well-crafted resume should make this expectation directly and explicitly.

There are many strategies, guidelines, and schools of thought related to how a resume should be written and presented. Resume are more an art than science, meaning that they are open to interpretation (art) rather than a set of rules and procedures that must be followed (science). In an environment where finding a job is becoming increasingly competitive and elusive, drafting the right resume assumes greater significance. Given its importance, there are some foundational strategies an applicant should consider that may present themselves, and their resume, in the best light. First is that since resumes—like cover letters—are written and presented with the intention of obtaining a job interview, then every word, phrase, bullet, and paragraph must be written in a style and manner that influences a human resource professional or recruiter to offer you an interview. First impressions are critical both in a prospective employer reading a resume and meeting a candidate. Ensure your resume has the necessary "wow" factor that garners the interest of its audience through it well-crafted and visually appealing authorship.

The second tactic of a well-drafted resume is to include, as referenced earlier, a short, direct statement conveying the career ambitions of the candidate. An applicant's career ambitions should be tailored and applicable to the position to which they are applying, and it should answer two questions: "Why has this applicant applied for this position?" and "Why is this organization the right one for this candidate." The career ambition statement, often titled "career focus" or "career objective," should also illuminate the singularly unique and noble ambition of a candidate, thus distinguishing one candidate from any others who might apply. Two examples of this approach would include:

- to utilize my decade-long experience serving in President ____'s White House
- to offer my skills and knowledge in producing more than 350 commercials for _____, the premier advertising and consulting agency in the United States.

For some candidates, the career focus section has been replaced by a skills or competency section, which highlights the skills or competencies a candidate possesses, often skills or competences related to the position they are applying for. These skills or competencies include statements such as "good team player," "expert communicator," and "solid decision-maker and problem-solver," all of which rarely influence a human resource professional or recruiter. Most expect this sector to be highly complementary about a person's qualifications; it would be the rare instance where a candidate states they have "acceptable team-building skills" or "average Microsoft Word abilities." Consequently, the "skills" section of a resume has lost some relevance and importance for those human resource professionals reviewing a resume and assessing the qualifications of an applicant. For those still seeking to include a skills section in their resume, they may consider combining the skills sector with their "career focus" or "career objective" sector, showing a clear and unambiguous ambition that is consistent with the direction of the organization. Here are three examples:

> Example 1: Hardworking and dedicated candidate seeking a long-term career with an innovative and community-centered organization dedicated to advancing—and balancing—the interests of its stakeholders with its commitment to serve the greater good of its community.

> Example 2: A smart, loyal, and outgoing candidate seeking to contribute to an organization on the cutting edge of science and technology, both of which will be utilized to raise the standard of living for those across the country and create a better world for its citizens to live.

Example 3: A talented and skilled professional, with an exceptional drive and attitude, seeks a sales position in an innovative organization that not only achieves spectacular success in its industry but also makes the world a better place to work and live.

These career objectives weave an applicant's skills and aptitudes within their ambitions, showcasing where they want to go and how they are going to get there. Moreover, candidates are promoting themselves as people who can help promote an organization. These objectives promote how this specific candidate can help that specific organization—by working collegially and collaboratively—raise its level of performance and better our world. This spotlights a candidate who is dedicated to more than their own professional success and personal aggrandizement. The candidate must utilize their position within the organization to create something unique, which is an organization that meets its objectives against its competitors and gives back to the community. It would be difficult to find an organization that would not be interested in the skills and aptitudes of a candidate of this caliber.

A third tactic of a powerful resume is one that is presented in a clear and direct manner. Each section of an applicant's history should be easy to find, with titles that are descriptive of the information that follows (for instance, "Work History," "Education," "Community Involvement," and "References"). Information should also be presented in a logical order to garner interest and ensure that information is presented in order of importance. If education is the most important aspect of an applicant's qualifications for a position, then it should be presented first. Conversely, if an organization is clearly seeking someone with significant experience in a particular area, that information should be included near the top/beginning of the resume.

The fourth strategy of more effective resumes is that they are constantly and continually updated, revised, and adapted. Critical to an applicant's eventual success in the application stage, a resume *must* be adapted and revised to ensure it is consistent with the qualifications and ambitions of the organizations to which a person is applying. There is no "one-size-fits-all" job, and there is not "one-size-fits-all" resume. Each resume should be reorganized and rewritten to address the expectations of your audience. If an organization is seeking someone with certain experiences or accomplishments, those experiences and accomplishments must be listed in a resume for the applicant to have a chance to continue in the process. As an example, an applicant's work experience should mirror that which an organization is seeking in potential employees.

Moreover, an applicant should use similar words and phrases in their resume to the ones that are used in the job announcement for the position they are applying for. In addition to mirroring an applicant's work experience to the requirements of the position to which they are applying, an applicant should ensure other aspects of their resume support their ambition to work at a particular organization. For instance, if there are certain community, civic, and professional organizations that are of interest to the organization to which an applicant is applying, they should ensure those organizations are included in the resume. Some organizations will only hire employees who are members of certain professional groups. As an example, many human resource professionals are members of the International Society of Human Resource Professionals, and many high-level health care employees are with the American Medical Association. Similarly, some organizations are highly philanthropic and look more favorably on a candidate who is a member of certain civil and community organizations, which may include the Salvation Army or the Boys and Girls Club. Hopefully, a human resource professional will view a resume and determine an applicant's history is a perfect match for the individual they seek because an applicant presents themselves as a perfect match for the position.

Without reservation, any words and phrases included in a resume must be accurate and a true reflection of an applicant's history. If your experience, education, achievements, and accomplishments are not consistent with or similar to the expectations of a prospective employer, then you cannot revise your resume to reflect those expectations. However, if an applicant's history is consistent and similar to the expectations of a prospective employer—but is written in a different manner, using different words and phrases—an applicant should consistent revising their resume to be more consistent with what an employer is hoping to read in a resume.

Organizations have different cultures and expectations of their employees, and those perceptions include how they view applicants and potential employees. Many organizations are looking for those who have a consistent and similar background, which includes how one presents themselves and their background in a resume. Therefore, resumes must reflect this differentiation. For this reason, the more successful applicants for a position have learned to adapt their resumes (including certain words and phrases) to the positions to which they are applying, modifying and revising appropriately 10–20 percent of their resumes for each and every position they apply.

The fifth strategy of the most influential resumes is the presentation of the applicant's experience. Arguably the most important aspect of a resume—mainly because past success is a barometer of future success—it is also the most misunderstood and misrepresented aspect of a resume. Applicants often fail to persuasively present their past accomplishments in a manner than foretells future accomplishments with their future employer. This can be a catastrophic error and a missed opportunity that prevents an applicant from continuing in the recruitment process.

When presenting a candidate's prior and current work experiences, the primary focus should be on accomplishments and not duties. Every position has duties and responsibilities, and all are listed in a job description or announcement. Restating those duties and responsibilities in a resume does not tell a prospective organization *how* a candidate performed those duties in their previous and current positions. It only shows that they performed the duties that were expected of them. The best presentation of a candidate's work experience should include a brief summary—one sentence or two—of a candidate's duties and responsibilities, followed by three to five bullets detailing the significant accomplishment achieved while serving in that position. These accomplishments should be among the most influential of a resume and be presented in a manner that foreshadows what this candidate can do for any organization they apply to.

In the end, most judge their lives by their accomplishments. Being a parent is not an accomplishment; instead, it is about how you raised your children and what they accomplished in their own lives. Serving thirty-four years in a particular organization is not the accomplishment remembered; it is that you built a new center to help disadvantaged children with their homework. It is said that all presidents of the United States can be summarized by a short, singular statement, such as one president who "ended the Cold War" or "opened China to the world." After all those years in office at the highest levels, these presidents are remembered for one or two achievements. It is an interesting reflection of one's many years in office.

This same approach should be taken an applicant reflecting upon their accomplishments in their previous or current employer. They should ask, "What did I do that will be remembered?" and "What accomplishments will future employers care the most about?" Once determined, those accomplishments should be presented in a manner where prospective employers will believe that their organization will similarly benefit from an applicant's talents. If a prospective employee is seeking a candidate who has experience creating a new sales program, the best candidate would have a statement in their resume from their past employment that states they "created a new sales program that increased sales 34 percent over a sixteen-month period." In reality, your work experience is not solely a record of your past accomplishments; instead, if written artfully, it will offer a prelude to what a candidate can do for any organization that chooses to hire them.

Accomplishments, like most sections of a resume, should be listed in order of influence and importance to a prospective employer. If building a new, million-dollar Teen Scene for the library is the most significant achievement of your tenure at the organization, or raising $2.5 million dollars over the course of four years, then those should be among the first bullets in the employment section of your resume. If the first or second bullet does not capture the interest of your audience, they may not read the third or fourth (there should only be four or six bullets listing an applicant's accomplishments for each position they have hold, with fewer bullets per employer if an applicant has had many employers and more bullets if an applicant has not had many employers). With few exceptions, the order of information and the manner in which that information is presented remain the paramount concerns for those crafting a resume.

A resume is the movie of your professional career, and like a movie, it should be visually stunning and intellectually captivating. It should move your audience and compel them to want to learn more about you, similar to watching the second episode of a television series or sequel to a movie. The best resumes are those that "hook" their audience to keep reading. Like a movie, a resume is virtually worthless unless someone views it. So, begin and end a resume with your audience in mind rather than an image or vision of yourself that you want to promote. An applicant should present themselves in a way that emphasizes their greatest accomplishments and minimizes their unfortunate disappointments, all targeted to meeting the expectations and demands of the audience. If an applicant can do so in a manner that fascinates their audience's heart, mind, and soul, they have a chance to write a box office smash.

A resume tells the story of your past—
an interview tells the promise of your future.

Performing in the Interview

Throughout the recruitment and selection process, both the potential employer and employee are being evaluated and judged. An organization may reflect upon a candidate and ask: Does the applicant have the proper education and experience? Are the applicant's background and qualifications consistent with the expectations? Will this applicant allow our organization to achieve our strategic objectives? Similarly, an applicant may reflect upon an organization and ask: Do I want to work at this firm, with their requirements, and within their culture? Will this job place me in a position to go where I want to go and to be what I want to be? All are important questions and lead both actors in the recruitment process to judge the worth and value of the opportunity that has been presented.

Without a doubt, the interview process remains a daunting and intimidating experience, mainly because we are judging and being judged by those we do not know well. Few can obtain a representative picture of another in a thirty-minute or sixty-minute interview. As some point, assumptions must be made based as much on perceptions and feelings as history and references. Only through extended and extensive time can one obtain a more complete view of a person or an organization.

No matter the process created or followed, there is an element of hope in the interview process. Applicants hope the interviewer is representing the organization fairly, so the applicant can make an informed judgement. An organization hopes the applicant has made an honest presentation of their strengths and weaknesses, in addition to their ambitions, so the organization can determine if this position best represents their interests. It is a challenging process for any actor in this play.

Of any step in the recruitment process, it is the interview that causes the most anxiety, and is the most judgmental, for several reasons. It is the first time the potential employer and potential employee meet in person; previously, each met only through written documentation or searches (a job announcement, a Google search, an application, a resume, or a cover letter). At this point, each is judged face-to-face, no longer hidden behind computers and papers. Biases and culture may play a role in this stage of the process, even for those who have been trained to control such beliefs and actions. For these reasons, the importance of the interview process cannot be overstated or underestimated.

Another reason the interview is so daunting is expectations. The applicant and the organization may have researched each party, completing documents (resume, cover letter) where the questions were known. In the interview, the applicant has less knowledge related to the specific questions that will be asked, raising the level of apprehension and nervousness. Then there are the perceptions built through the process thus far and that each side to the interview is hoping to answer: Will I like those I interview with? Can this candidate really be this good? Is this a place where I really want to work? These are unanswerable questions before an interview, causing some degree of stress before and during the interview, with the hope that each side in the interview represented themselves and/or their organization comprehensively, fairly, and honestly.

Without a doubt, the greatest burden and stress in the interview process lies with the applicant. At this stage, the applicant does not have a job or has a job and is searching for a better one. Therefore, there is more to risk, and to gain, in the interview process for the applicant than the recruiter. Crafting a plan to minimize these stresses and excel in the process may lie at the heart of eventual success in any recruitment process, and an applicant may consider certain strategies to alleviate some of that anxiety and perform well in the interview process.

The first action to best prepare for an interview is to study, study, study, and then study more. It was once said, "Presentation without preparation always leads to devastation." An interview is a test in the employment sector, and similar to most tests in school, there are few who do well without studying. Those best prepared for the interview, and who best present themselves in an interview, are those who have thoroughly researched their interviewer, from the job announcement to the job description, from interviewing past and current employees to various stakeholders such as investors and vendors. Study, and you are better prepared, and if you are better prepared, you have more confidence.

Through this investigatory process, you may learn how the organization wants to be viewed by others and how they are really viewed by those they interact with and do business with, including those who have a vested stake in their future (such as other employees and customers). In this stage of the process, an applicant determines the potential questions that should be asked of the interviewers and the organization. The questions asked by the applicant to those on the interview panel are often among the more important since the interview panel may not have prepared an answer for the question and, consequently, may give a more personal/forthright answer. In general, an applicant should ask at least one question upon the conclusion of an interview, and this question should not request information that the applicant should have obtained before the interview (for instance, how many employees work in the organization or the main focus of the company's strategic plan if that plan is already public). Several questions an applicant may consider asking of the interview panel include:

- If you could change one aspect of this organization to make it a better place to work, what would that be? (This is a chance for the applicant to become aware of current employee issues for someone working at the organization).
- If this organization could only invest in either more technology or more employees, but not both, what would

this organization invest in? (This will detail the focus of an organization's research and development monies, along with the value they place on future employ growth and, possibly, promotional opportunities).

- If you could build the perfect employee for this position, what one skill or aptitude would they possess? (This gives the applicant a sense of what the interview panel is truly looking for, and it gives the applicant a chance to highlight their skill in this particular area).

The second strategy that allows a candidate to excel in the interview process is to *get them to like you.* An employment interview serves two purposes: to verify the qualifications an applicant listed in their resume and cover letter and to determine whether the candidate would be the best addition to the organizational team. Organizations want to hire an applicant who advances their interests, of course, but also the candidate whose personality and attitude are extraordinarily positive, who is personable and generous, and who displays a genuine kindness to every person they meet.

How best can you get someone to like you? A great start is a genuine smile along with a firm handshake (if culturally acceptable) when you first meet someone. Being attentive to the questions asked and presenting thoughtful answers continues this positive exchange. It is perfectly acceptable to write notes when a question is asked to ensure that all aspects of the question are answered and to ask the interview panel if the question was fully answered. Finally, we tend to like those who are considerate and kind, so applicants who are considerate of the interview panel's time and relay their gratitude for the opportunity extended is appreciated. Sincerely thank the interviewer for their time, in a warm and polite manner, to be followed almost immediately with a handwritten note expressing the candidate's appreciation for the interview panel's kindness and consideration.

Kindness, as has and will be expressed throughout this book, is one of those few traits that place an individual in a position to be seen in respectful and laudatory terms. More than nearly any other personal trait, there are few circumstances that cannot be overcome by someone who is kind and considerate, who treats others better than they are treated, and who displays a positive and warm personality no matter the challenges faced. This is a trait that best allows a candidate, or a person, to present themselves well in an interview or any social setting, and this may be the attribute that ultimately ensures an interview is more memorable than others who may apply and be interviewed who do not possess this trait.

The third strategy for those who succeed in an interview is the ability to *nail two specific questions.* These two questions are almost always asked of an interviewee in an interview, and an applicant should expect they will be asked: Why does the applicant want the job? Why is the applicant the best person for the job? Prospective employers want to know why an applicant has applied for the position, including the general and specific interest that this position has in the short- and long-term ambitions of the applicant. Employers do not want to be the "transition position" in an applicant's career; instead, an organization is searching for an applicant they can invest considerable training monies and developmental effort into with the hopes that an employee's superior performance will enable the organization to achieve its strategic ambition and direction.

Applicants should have a good idea why they want the job before they apply for the position at the organization. Moreover, the "why I want this job" statement should be included in the resume under "Career Focus" or "Career Objective." Applicants should have a firm understanding of why they applied for the position before the interview, and the answer to that question should be thoroughly researched and easily related to the interview panel once asked. The second question, too, should be easily answered by an applicant since they should have determined what the organization is looking for in this position and how the candidate's combination of skills and abilities meet—and exceed—these expectations. Whether this question is asked or not, an applicant should never leave an interview without clearly stating—over any other person who may apply for the position—why they are the best skilled, knowledgeable, motivated, and able applicant for the job. The candidate should not let the interview panel determine if they are the most qualified for the position; the answer, by the candidate, to this question should clearly and unquestionable state why the candidate is the best, and only, person for the position.

The answer to this question solely relates to the qualifications an applicant possesses and the qualifications the candidate will utilize to add significantly to the success of the organization. This is the opportunity for an applicant to overtly and specifically "sell" themselves to the interview, to relate every reason the organization would be most unwise not to hire them for the position. The applicant's answer should relay every single reason the organization should hire them for the position—and do so in an expedited manner.

Interviewees who cannot answer why they want the job, and why they should be hired for the job, rarely are offered the job. Considerable time and attention should be devoted to ensuring the interviewee has a solid and compelling history and story that answers these two critical questions.

The fourth trait of those who do best in the interview is being confident. Confidence comes from being proud of past accomplishments and convinced of future achievements. Employees want an applicant who displays a respectful yet warranted degree of confidence. As my father once said, "If you do not have confidence in yourself, how can you expect anyone else to have confidence in you?" If you have confidence in your future, your potential employer will have greater confidence in their own future because, once you are hired, they believe you will achieve what you promise.

Undoubtedly, developing confidence in an employment interview can be a challenge, especially when most perceive the power in an interview rests primarily with the employer. Most people meet lack confidence in some part of their lives; the successful ones have simply learned to control or overcome it. There are other strategies an applicant may consider to raise their confidence level during an interview:

- First is to remember that there are millions of other jobs across the globe, some of them better than the one the applicant is applying for and others not as good. There are also positions that may be better aligned to an applicant's background and ambitions. If an applicant is not chosen for this position, through patience and persistence, another position will almost certainly present itself.

- Second is that confidence comes from the realization that a person has something important to say and to contribute. Believe in the inherent value and worth to yourself, and that self-assurance will propel a candidate through nearly any challenging or contentious situation that may be faced.
- Third is that the nervousness and conflict within an interview often arises because an interviewee believes they are being judged by another person or the organization. If you do not care what others think, the stress of being "judged" is eviscerated. Be a good person and do the right thing—and then never care what others think. They can only affect how you feel and how you present yourself, which can be debilitating in almost any situation, including an interview.

One develops confidence to excel in an interview by recognizing that this is only one job among many, and one interview among a series of conversations an applicant will have in their employment career. Interviewees develop confidence by realizing they have something important to say and something valuable to contribute, and this position offers both the interviewee and the interviewer that opportunity. Finally, confidence is gained when a person believes they are a good, decent, and honorable person, and no matter what happens in an interview, that perception and realization is never changed or affected. That is how confidence is developed, and the confidence helps you nail almost any interview you choose to seek.

The final strategy to do well in an interview is to at least get into the game. One cannot be interviewed unless they apply, and one cannot be hired unless they are interviewed. It is almost impossible to win unless you compete. You must be in the arena to have a chance. That may mean you lose some, and in today's market, you will most likely lose many more times than you win. But you can never test your abilities, to prove your capabilities, unless you roll the dice and get in the game. In the employment sector, "getting in the game" means you have to at least apply, at least interview, at least take the chance.

An often-asked question is what position a person should apply and interview for, and which are beyond the limits of a certain strategy or formula. One can never predict, with absolute certainty, the competition for certain positions or the true character of an organization. There is a degree of chance and luck in most of what do (though some of that chance and luck can be mitigated through the strategies contained in this book). But no process if foolproof or certain of success.

Determining where, and when, to apply for a position is both an art and a science. On one hand, you never truly know a position until you apply and interview, during which more information about the position can be garnered. Moreover, as previously stated, an applicant does not know the level of competition for the position or the specific questions of the interview panel, all of which can be determined as one progresses through the interview process. One the other hand, applying for a position when there is little chance a position would be accepted (for instance, the salary is too low or the job is located too far from an applicant's desired living location) should be avoided at all costs since you may prevent other, more serious applicants from continuing in the process.

When should an applicant apply for a position? In general, a person should apply for a position if they meet the qualifications, if there are no insurmountable barriers to accepting the position, and if they have a real and genuine interest in accepting the offer should it be extended. There is much to learn about an organization in the interview process; this information will enable a candidate to make a more informed decision. Moreover, applying for a position does strengthen an applicant's skills in crafting a cover letter and resume and performing during an interview.

An applicant should not, however, apply and interview for a position if they do not intend on accepting the position if offered (given the information obtained from the interview process about the position and the organization is consistent with expectations). If an applicant has little interest in accepting the position, they may take an interview position from someone who has a genuine interest in the position, and that should be avoided. Applying for a position though an applicant may have some reservations (e.g., you may be seeking additional wages or the work hours may be challenging) is perfectly acceptable since those questions can be discussed in the interview process, hopefully earlier in the process rather than later.

An applicant who has an interest in a position should always apply. Even in those circumstances where they may not have the level of education, experience, and skills sought by the employer, an applicant may have specific education and experiences that are particularly valued by an employer and may end up being more successful in the process than originally thought. Additionally, the interview process may highlight other positions in the organizations that an applicant may be better qualified for, and the interview process may prompt the organization to recommend an applicant apply for a different position. As I often tell my children, Gunner and Tori, never tell yourself no. At least step up to the plate and get into the game; let someone else tell you no.

Some years ago, I applied for a position at an organization I thought was perfect for my career. During the interview process, the conversation moved from the position I was applying for to a more senior position. Following the interview, I was asked if I was interested in that higher position, which offered more responsibilities and a considerably higher salary. I accepted that position and was fortunate that the interview process resulted in a position more aligned with my skills and ambitions, along with those of the organization. So, the application process and interview may not result in receiving the position, but it may lay the groundwork for working within that organization in another capacity at some point in the future.

In this life, we have seen that the inevitable inevitably happens. It is not possible to predict with absolute certainty the advent of industry and employment. The world is simply changing too rapidly because of astonishing advances in technology and evolving social mores and customs around the globe. Those who explore and research the probable future and then prepare for its eventuality are traveling along the right road. That road may not be smooth, paved with the best of intentions of those met along the way, or even constructed, but it is traveled by those who realize that their present location and situation offer little hope of something better.

Throughout the world, millions of people move from one country to another with a sense of optimism and an idealized hope that something different may indeed be something better. They have a solid appreciation of the past and an understanding of the future, from the promises to the perils, and they know the unexpected often happens in unsettling times. They soldier on, building and enhancing their capabilities and abilities to position themselves to profit from both the expected and the unexpected.

One of the foundations that best positions a person to excel during such times is the relationships they build, develop, and maintain. Such relationships, if built in an honest and sincere fashion, can tie individuals into networks that can be utilized to better find, and ultimately be successful in, the job markets that may arise. It is these relationships, culminating in an intricate web of personal and employment networks, that we next turn our attention to in the hopes of positioning ourselves in the right place to find the right job.

If you have common skills, you get common pay;
if you have uncommon skills, you get uncommon pay.

Building Relationships

We have seen that technology has radically altered the method and manner in which we search for jobs today. Decades ago, positions were advertised through local or regional newspapers since the newspaper was the focal point for advertising for vacant positions and news in general. Those who wanted to search for positions outside of their local geographic region confronted an arduous, time-consuming, and expensive venture. That contrasts sharply with the method in which people obtain their information today. There are countless options for obtaining news today. From Facebook to Twitter to the literally thousands of smartphone apps that deliver news (often unfiltered and unresearched, and at times biased). There is no longer one source or destination for obtaining news and information—let alone the information on available job opportunities.

In any country, dozens of websites advertise positions throughout that country and the world. They advertise and publicize thousands of jobs in nearly every industry an applicant can consider. One employment website has more than 200 million visitors each month, and those visitors come from more than sixty countries. This mechanism has taken the place of newspapers—to the benefit of the employer and applicant. Employers find it much simpler, and less expensive, to advertise to a wider audience; applicants, likewise, can find information on nearly any job opportunity that exists in almost any industry. There are trade associations, employment agencies, and employment-related search engines that are specifically created to entice prospective applicants to visit their website (some websites charge employers a fee to advertise open positions, and others charge advertisers a fee to sell their products to those who visit the website).

To be sure, and to the benefit of almost everyone, searching for jobs to apply for has never been easier or more global. One may believe actually securing the perfect job, or the good job, has never been easier too, but as we have learned, they would be mistaken. Unfortunately, finding prospective jobs to apply for is easier for the applicant, but it is also easier for the millions more who now have access to the same pool of positions. In the past, looking for a job was a more regional pursuit. Applicants typically searched for positions in their town or county, but today, the ease of locating open employment positions on the internet has made the applicant and interview process a more global adventure. Countless more applications are added to recruitments, and competition has rarely been so intense. The odds of obtaining an interview through the submission of a resume and cover letter—no matter how effectively and artfully written—are not high. The greater odds of obtaining an interview, and the position, fall to those who build relationships among all they meet, who network far and wide throughout their industry, and create, build, and sustain those relationships over the long term.

Studies indicate networking and building relationships play a vital role in obtaining a job, possibly even the central role. The ability to develop relationships between a person seeking a job and a person who can assist a person in securing a job is at the heart of success in seeking employment. Networking and the building of relationships play a leading role in obtaining employment—far more than thought by many in the job market today. Many prominent studies have reinforced the importance of utilizing networks to secure employment:

- The US Bureau of Labor Statistics and Yale University (2016) reported in a combined study that 70 percent of all jobs are found through networking. A similar study, this one by

Doyle (2017), found that 60 percent of jobs are found through networking.

- Brown, Setren, and Topa (2014) found that approximately 30 to 50 percent of applicants were hired through referrals from current employees.
- Adler (2016) highlighted a LinkedIn study that showed those casually looking for a job were three times more likely— and those not actively looking for a job were seven times more likely—to find a job through networking than directly applying for a job.
- Crispin and Mehler (2014) of Career Roads concluded that only 15 percent of positions were filled through job boards, with most jobs filled through internal recommendations or other referrals.
- CareerBuilder (2015) surveyed more than two thousand hiring managers and concluded more than 70 percent look first at referrals and internal networks before posting a position to the wider public. This is a critical statistic because it implies, if not outwardly states, that many job opportunities are not advertised and/or publicized. They are filled by applicants and employees within a given network, thereby precluding any recruitment process.

Relationships and networking play a role in securing future employment, and that role is expected to rise unabated in the future. Given the lack of security, stability, and permanence in today's turbulent job market, the ability to create relationships with friends, coworkers, neighbors, college alumni, business associates, fellow association members, family friends, hobby groups, children's associations (Little League, Girl Scouts, etc.), community and civic board attendees, church members, former employers and coworkers, and social acquaintances—virtually anyone you come in contact with in your everyday life—are the key to success in finding employment. The more acquaintances an applicant knows and is affiliated with— the more names one has in their Rolodex—the better chance one may have of becoming aware of job opportunities, whether those opportunities are publicly announced or not.

To be sure, relationships and networking do not automatically translate into obtaining the next jo or the best job. It does, however, present the possibility that you will become more aware of job possibilities that exist, and thus present an applicant with at least the opportunity to inquire about the position if not actually submit a letter of interest or an employment application. Opportunities do not always lead to success, but it is difficult to foresee how success can be achieved without at least having the opportunity.

Without a doubt, developing and sustaining relationships that may be utilized in an applicant's job aspirations is a challenge, mainly because of the time and effort it consumes. Many job applicants have a current job that demands their attention, a family to support, and other outside interests that require some commitment and attention. However, the proper time, effort, commitment, and attention must be found and then invested in building relationships that are mutually beneficial, personally enriching, and professionally rewarding. Without these relationships, an applicant—as mentioned previously—may not become aware of up to 70 percent of all job opportunities, a figure that amounts to millions of job opportunities annually, or quite possibly the one job they most covet and have the perfect background to excel at. Thus, the importance of creating and sustaining personal and professional relationships is of paramount concern to those in the workplace today. How can these networks be created? How can these relationships be maintained? At best, by following three strategies, each discussed in greater detail in the following pages:

Meeting as Many People as Possible

While you cannot meet everyone or be a member of everything, you can invest in yourself by joining as many clubs and groups as possible. It is nearly impossible to build relationships unless you are in the arena, meeting a wide array of people. This is, undoubtedly, the most time-consuming aspect of finding and retaining a job, but relationships take time to create and even more time to maintain. But, if networks and relationships offer a high chance of success in the recruitment and selection process, then devoting extra time to this venture will not be wasted or be in vain. It does take time to join a range of clubs, groups, associations, and committees—and even more to invest in building and preserving relationships with those you meet. However, you never know when the next group you join, or the next person within the group you join, will be the individual who has that unique contact or entry into the industry or position that is of interest to you.

Relationships and networking have proven successful because an applicant may become aware of potential employment and promotional opportunities, and an applicant may also become more of a "known quantity" to the hiring organization. If a hiring organization has a positive relationship with an individual, and that individual recommends an applicant within their network to that organization, then the applicant is now more familiar to the organization. This personal contact or connection with an applicant may raise the confidence of the organization into actually knowing "who" the applicant is and whether the applicant would be a good candidate for the position. With some exceptions, applicants who have been referred to an organization by individuals the organization trusts are often considered to a greater degree than those who apply when the organization is unaware of their history and potential future.

This is why relationships can play a key part in the recruitment process. Recruiters and employers invest a considerable amount of resources in selecting someone to join their organization, and they look for assurances that the person selected will be the right person, at the right time, and for the right reasons. Those assurances do come over time: the more time you spend with someone, the more you trust what they believe, how they will act, and what they will do. Potential employers learn—through time and experience—whether potential employees believe in the same philosophies they do, how they will act and react in a given situation, and the effort they will expend and commitment they will devote to meet their obligations. If an organization can learn about a candidate's past and potential from someone they trust, they are more likely to be comfortable with making the difficult decision to choose a referred candidate over one they do not have a relationship with.

Relationships are not easy, and they do take time, but once developed, each party in the relationship has a degree of trust in who the other person is, including their interests and ambitions. We learn as much about ourselves as we do others, and with that knowledge, we can better determine whether we want to be associated with certain individuals or organizations. Undoubtedly, we gravitate toward those with similar philosophies, and the same is true for the organizations we choose to work for and with. Developing relationships aids our pursuit of who we are and where we want to go, and it helps identifying individuals who can help us along that road. On that road, our hope is that these relationships aid us in the recruitment and selection process, giving us a chance to show an organization that we are the person they need to make their organization a success. A perfect opportunity for that to occur is before a position is open and advertised.

If, through the networks that are formed, an applicant can interact with potential employers, then an employer may see an applicant for who they really are—without the assumption that they are "acting" in order to become the type of person the employer is seeking. The organization, too, can make a more informed determination as to whether the individual may be the right person for a potential position. For example, joining the chamber of commerce, Lyons Club, or Rotary Club allows a potential job applicant to meet a host of individuals and organizations who, at some point in the future, may be searching for a person with their particular qualifications. Had they not joined one of those clubs, become an active and valued contributor to its success, and developed that network of relationships, certain employment opportunities may not have come their way.

Relationships start with joining as many organizations and clubs as possible and then interacting with as many people as is conceivable with the hope that in some of those interactions, a person can build positive and constructive relationships among those met, including those who may offer professional advice and assistance to a candidate and their career. Without placing oneself in that position, a person cannot learn about, and then take advantage of, opportunities that come one's way.

Qualifications may garner you an interview,
but likeability will garner you the job.

Being the Person People Want to Meet, Know, and Spend Time With

As we can imagine, it is not possible to know "who a person truly is" through a recruitment interview or even a series of interviews. Each participant in the recruitment process is acting to some degree, trying to portray a better version of themselves. The employer wants the best applicant to believe their organization is stable yet aggressive, with unbounded growth over the horizon; the employee wants the best employer to believe they are the hardest worker with the greatest ideas, with virtually limitless potential to realize their dreams. Moreover, each actor in the interview interprets the other through their own lenses and perceptions. An interviewee may believe they are portraying an image of a conscientious professional, whereas the employee may see an overconfident and inflexible team member. Similarly, the organization may believe they are portraying a fun place to work, yet the applicant may interpret their interview questions as rigid and dogmatic.

Each actor is trying to present the best version of their history and the most optimistic version of their future. They are striving to create a credible and convincing performance that prompts the other participants in the process to conclude that they "really like this person" or "really want to work with this company." One is, in essence, trying to get the other to "like" them because whether it is hamburgers or chocolate, reading or traveling, what someone likes causes them to have a more optimistic attitude toward it. If an applicant interviewing for a position, or an organization interviewing a potential employee, is liked by the other, then they will be seen in a brighter light, often irrespective of any deficiencies and disadvantages that may arise in the process.

Likeability permeates nearly any relationship we create, build, or sustain. We create relationships because we want to meet someone, build relationships because we want to know someone, and sustain relationships because we want to spend time with someone. Be the person people want to meet, know, and spend time with—and your relationships will stand the test of time. How does one become this type of person? What are the traits, characteristics, and strategies one should consider that will make them a more likeable person? There are, of course, many traits and strategies that one should consider, but there are three that are among the most important. First, the most likeable persons are those who are happy and optimistic. People and organizations want to associate with those who make them feel good and who can give a shine to an otherwise dull or opaque day. People like what makes them feel good, whether it is a smile from an acquaintance or an encouraging word from a friend. They make us feel better about ourselves and our situations, and for that reason, we want to continually associate with these individuals.

The second trait that leads to one becoming a likeable person is a sense of honesty and sincerity. There are those who spend their lives trying to become better versions of who they are: to tell the truth more often, to forgive those who have injured them, and to help others without the expectation of a reward or recognition. These are actions that are admirable, appreciated, and respected if done with an open and conscientious heart.

Relationships built upon false premises or promises rarely last. The applicant for a position who portrays a different (or better) version of who they really are eventually is exposed, often to their detriment. The applicant realizes the knowledges and skills they presented in the interview are not capabilities they possess in order to succeed in the position. The organization, too, becomes aware they selected the wrong person for the position: the candidate who was presented in the interview is not the same employee selected for the position. At this point, the employment relationship is often severed, and the organization has to begin the recruitment process again, at considerable expense. Compounding the gravity of the situation for the employee is that they may have resigned a previous position to accept the new position, and now the employee has lost a second position, all because the candidate was not truthful in the recruitment process. A person was challenged to present a picture of themselves that is not true; eventually, one's real personality arises, and if that persona conflicts with what was presented earlier, eventually that mistake is corrected, to the detriment of the applicant and the organization.

What does last is presenting who a person is and who a person strives to become in an honest and forthright manner. Most ache for something or someone who is sincere, someone who presents their advantages and disadvantages, strengths and weaknesses, and confidences and fears. You will rarely meet someone who is not challenged by some circumstance; some try to overcome those challenges, and others try to accept them. In both cases, those who present themselves as who they are, rather than who they want to be, are those who can better establish and strengthen relationships with others. Rare is the person without burdens or faults, yet being honest and sincere about your past and present, hopes and dreams, creates a bond with those who live in a similar world, which encompasses most of those we know.

Finally, those who are liked often give more than they get. A foundational element of relationships is sharing, and a person who continually asks, wants, and takes from others without reciprocity damages the relationship—often beyond repair. One may feel taken advantage of, even used, and lose interest in continuing the relationship. In the best relationships, both people feel enriched and rewarded, even though one may seemingly receive more benefit than the other. Think of the other person as much, if not more, than you think of yourself. Give as much, if not more, than you get, and you will be forever rewarded through the type of relationship you create, build, and maintain in your personal and professional lives.

Building Relationships That Last

As we have learned, those working today are going to spend fewer years with their current employers and have more jobs throughout their careers than previous generations. We may not travel from employer to employer, or job to job, on a yearly basis, but the days when a person will devote twenty to thirty years with the same employer are over. Most organizations do not last long, causing loyalty between an employer and their employees to become more rare, especially as globalization has brought countless competitors into the marketplace. Stability and security no longer exist between producers and the consumers they serve, causing stability and security to falter between employees and the employers they serve.

We live in a transitory world that is marked by fluidity rather than constancy. In these uncertain times, we look for some sort of predictability and permanence to ease our trepidations and stabilize our lives. Relationships offer that opportunity, and relationships that last through both rewarding and troubling times offer comfort and joy that is rarely found in any other manner. This is especially true with relationships formed to advance one's professional aspirations. To build and sustain relationships with those who can offer wise advice and constructive guidance as to where a person should seek employment, and whom one may contact in this endeavor, is essential for long-term professional stability and security.

Building relationships may be a challenge, but sustaining relationships is the greater challenge. There is a tendency to create relationships when they are needed and terminate relationships when they appear unneeded or unnecessary. In the professional realm—where one is never confident in their present, let alone their future—the need to create and preserve relationships over time is central. The need to build relationships that last, that neither fade or falter, requires genuine desire, considerable time, and conscious effort. Monthly texts to ensure continuity, bimonthly emails to ensure current statuses are shared, quarterly phone calls to solicit advice, and semiannual meetings over coffee or lunch to express appreciation are actions that, at a minimum, should be considered. There are other strategies to consider, which may include personal cards, letters, and small gifts that showcase one's gratitude and appreciation to another who is a critical factor in their future. All, of course, should be done with the utmost in sincerity.

Some of the more challenging relationships to manage are those where another person has damaged your reputation or future. This may be a coworker or supervisor, someone who is challenged to be a good and decent person. They may injure you and your ambitions for reasons not for who you are, but for who they are. They may be jealous, envious, and greedy, seeking to dismiss, degrade, and disparage you and those in your life. They are unfortunate souls living tortured lives. Responding in kind can be destructive to one's career. In doing so, one has become the same person as the tortured one. Others may see the type of person you have become, albeit in response to how unfortunately other may treat you rather than the better person you can become.

Those who attempt to damage your career may not succeed, but you could damage your own career depending on how you respond. Rise above the petty and disparaging actions others may direct toward you and work to become the better person. It is a characteristic among the most admirable in others—to respond to the negative with the positive, and the bad with the good. Adopting that trait and becoming that type of person, may become the foundation of long-term, stable relationships with others. This applies to those one has worked with in the past, work with in the present, and hope to work with in the future.

In summary, repeated contact, continual communications, and endless consultations are strategies that sustain relationships, and all arise through the knowledge that relationships take a genuine desire to create, considerable time to develop, and a conscious effort to maintain. Those individuals who can, and ultimately do, build and maintain these networks and relationships attain security in their professional ambitions and stability in their personal aspirations.

Customers are too fickle,
technology is too advanced,
and economies are too fragile
to create industries and jobs that last.

Never Stop Looking for a Job

The final strategy to finding and retaining the right job is to never stop looking for the right job. Similar to relationships, jobs will not last for those in the workplace today: organizations do not remain in business as long as those that existed in 1920s or the 1950s, goods can be made in nearly any corner of the world by almost any organization (and often at a lower price), and science and technology continue to make many of the products and services we use obsolete. The good job, as we have learned, will not last, no matter how much we like what we do and enjoy what we create. The perfect job of today is rapidly becoming the obsolete job of tomorrow.

Finding and retaining a job rests on a number of pillars, and two of the most important are work and time. You must work hard to find a job, work harder to retain that job, and then—since your current job will surely not last—work hardest to find your next job. If you are not looking forward to your next job, you will be looking backward to your last. For those searching for some sort of professional security, then obtaining, retaining, and finding a job will consume exponentially more of your personal life in terms of time, effort, and money. Those rewarded with professional stability are those who are willing to sacrifice the time, devote the effort, and pay the price that is a necessity to survive—not just succeed—in today's volatile world, a world where applicants and employees compete against humans, robots, and artificial intelligence.

Consequently, looking for a job has actually *become* a job. The most successful in the job market today are those who do something every day to find the next job, no matter how rewarding or profitable their current job may be. They study the histories of the past, are aware of the realities of the present, and prepare for the inevitability of the future. They become aware of economic trends, investigate forthcoming industries, create contacts in creative organizations, and apply for opportunities with new employers. No matter whether that future is advantageous or welcome, they regrettably accept what was, never settle for what is, and look forward to what can be. They realize that very little lasts through time and what is good is often gone, and they are willing to rethink and retrain, to reconceptualize and restructure, to reimagine and rebuild and create a more secure destiny.

These are the ones who work hard and invest their time, knowing that preparing for what is next offers more promise than lamenting what is past. Though recognition, acceptance, and anticipation, they become the most willing, the most capable, and the most adaptable, and the ones who profit most in an uncompromising and even hostile world.

Summary

You need a reason to get up in the morning.

Every few generations, the world changes in profound ways. Changes of this magnitude follow advances in communication (the telegraph, telephone), technology (the printing press, the cotton gin, Facebook), medicine (penicillin, polio vaccine), wars (Napoleonic Wars, Russian Civil War, World War I and II), and transportation (trains, automobiles, airplanes) that alter our very way of life. The early decades of the twenty-first century may be another tectonic shift in world history. On one hand, advances in communication, technology, medicine, and transportation have afforded many of the world's inhabitants a standard of living few imagined; on the other, the same advances are decimating a person's ability to obtain and retain employment.

In the midst of unparalleled progress, a growing sense of anxiety and uncertainty pervade a generation unable to find the good job, losing their future to the growing army of robots that work better and cheaper than humans, and with artificial intelligence created to think faster, and more intelligently, than humans ever could. It is an ironic twist of fate: the very technology we designed to create a more advanced society is now on the precipice of destroying the employment opportunities for a generation.

Without a job to make a living, and a profession to build a future, a person is without the financial and societal resources to participate in society, let alone contribute to its development. The good job has become hard to find and difficult to keep, but those with the right ambitions—who explore the future to identify the possibilities that may exist, who are best prepared and interview for the next generation of jobs, who build relationships with anyone and everyone they meet, and who never stop looking for a job—are the ones who good fortune shines upon.

The average number of years a person has been in their current job continues to fall, and the average number of jobs a person will have over their lifetime continues to rise. Wages have barely moved since the mid-1970s, and manufacturing industries have actively moved overseas since the 1970s. Business after business, market after market, and industry after industry have revolutionized their production processes to become more efficient and effective, most often by using technology to eliminate employees. Consequently, nearly any statistic produced depicts an economy unable to produce the number of good jobs, from the highest educated to the lowest skilled, that offer the hope for a better life. But there is a ray of hope for those who have learned how to find the right type of job and for those who have learned how to become the right type of employee.

The great have a talent that is uncommon,
an idea that is unrivaled,
a confidence that is unshakable,
and a determination that is unwavering.

3

BEING THE RIGHT EMPLOYEE

We will never achieve all we strive to do,
nor become everything we aspire to become,
but we must do something
with the belief that we can become anything.

Throughout history, citizens born in nearly any generation claim they live in challenging times. Whether it's wars or depressions, homelessness or unhappiness, famines or diseases, each generation does face their own "historic" challenge. Some face this peril with dogged determination, hard work, sacrifice, and a confidence that through commitment and dedication, practically any challenge can be overcome, almost any obstacle beaten, nearly any foe defeated, and virtually every ambition realized. While some tests and trials are certainly on the historic end of the continuum—the American Revolution in the 1770s, the Civil War in the 1860s, and the Great Depression in the 1920s and 1930s—the economical and societal challenges facing this generation have the possibility to utterly transform the way we work and live.

Time will tell, but a principal challenge confronting this generation—the ability to find the good job, with a good salary and solid benefits that offer the promise of security and stability in our lives—will revolutionize our very way of life. Average citizens are confronting questions, bordering on doubts, about how one can make a living or provide the basic necessities to raise oneself and a family. What are the jobs of the future (or the jobs of the present)?

Where will the jobs of tomorrow be? How can I garner the knowledge and skills to be a qualified person to obtain that job? How can I compete against robots and machines that work faster and cheaper than any human can? Machines have alleviated many of the physical requirements needed to perform jobs, and technology has eliminated many of those that remain. Robots are producing an increasingly high percentage of the cars, tractors, and televisions that are made today, and that percentage is projected to increase at an alarming rate. Today, nearly anything made today is produced, either in part or in whole, through the utilization of computers and robots.

In the coming years, products and services thought incapable of being produced by anything other than employees will be overtaken by the dramatic advances in science and technology. Robots will drive cars (no more Uber and Lyft), build houses (decimating one of the most secure sources of employment for millions), and patrol streets (human police officers may become a relic of a bygone time in history). Artificial intelligence has assumed a greater role in those jobs requiring intellectual aptitude from designing skyscrapers to interpreting x-rays and filing tax returns. Missions to space will be designed by artificial intelligence and then use robots to travel to it, similar to artificial intelligence designing the curriculum in our schools and then using robots to present it.

It is an interesting conundrum. The robots and artificial intelligence created to make life easier, and the world better, have now assumed the power to create a future—in some ways—that is disadvantageous to the economic progress of those who created it. Jobs and employment prospects are gone, without the conceivable prospect that they may return. In fact, virtually everything an employee does today will be done differently in the next decade, and often not by other employees. Those who remain employed will be required to act and think differently, in a more demanding, expansive, and intellectually sound and complex manner. In particular, the jobs of the future will require employees to acquire a set of characteristics, abilities, and ambitions common to some, foreign to others, but collectively offer the best chance to attain a sense of security and stability in an increasingly chaotic and frenzied workplace. The most prominent of these characteristics, abilities, and ambitions are:

- working hard
- thinking differently
- adapting and adjust
- being loyal and caring

Work Hard

Work hard on work that matters.

My grandmother, Elizabeth "Vee" McCoy, taught me an important lesson that has inspired nearly every action of my life, from high school to college, raising a family to teaching college. She taught me to work hard on work that matters. The lesson always centered around the need to work hard at anything and everything you did. She knew of few individuals who became a somebody or achieved something who did not have, at their core being, the willingness and ability to work hard.

I learned another important lesson from my grandmother and my parents: working hard is a trait of the good, but working hard on something that matters is a trait of the great. I was taught to use whatever unique skills and uncommon talents I possessed to work hard on something that matters. The happy person is one who finds work that is important to them and valued by others, and then devotes their time and efforts to working hard at that type of work because it is worth doing.

My grandmother had a keen insight, developed generations ago, that one gains meaning in life not by participating but by contributing. Those who contribute their unique knowledge and skills to the betterment of themselves and others will live lives of purpose and have meaning in the time they spend on earth. She was a special person who influenced my ambitions to a great degree, especially through her continual lesson that the journey may start with work that matters, but little of importance, value, or meaning can be achieved unless you work hard. Working hard is more than showing up to work on time, completing what is requested, and performing what is required. Doing what is requested or required is no longer enough; a person must do more if they want to become more.

At a minimum, our world demands more time, more effort, and more initiative. Organizations want applicants with motivation, who show the inventiveness that may make the organization's product or service cheaper and more attractive to its customers. Supervisors expect employees to work eight hours in the office—followed by another hour or two answering emails and texts at home. Managers expect employees to complete their responsibilities and assist their coworkers and supervisors in completing their responsibilities too so that the division and organizational is more productive and profitable. Organizations, supervisors, and managers demand that employees display creativity and ingenuity, solving conflicts before they become concerns and issues before they become problems, with the hopes that an organization has a chance to be more effective with their products and more efficient with their processes. Little, if any, of the above is accomplished unless an employee and the organization work hard first.

These are the expectations of an employee who wants a chance to remain employed. For those who cannot meet these expectations, a legion of applicants is waiting to take their place. But most want more than a chance to remain employed—or the chance to follow their dreams. They want to advance in their organization, secure higher-level and higher-paying positions in better organizations, move to more secure professions and industries, or quite possibly create their own business, one that affords them greater control over their future career. Those who made it did so because they worked hard, believing that through their hard work that the battle could be won, and that their dream could be realized. That belief in work and oneself is common to us all; what is uncommon is those who actually did something with it, and here are a few who did just that.

Tyler Perry

Tyler Perry was abused as a child, and as a youth, he tried to commit suicide. He later wrote a play that failed miserably, but that did not detour him from his dream. He took odd jobs to support his quest to write the great American play, and finally he did. Years later, he topped the *Forbes* list of the highest-earning entertainers after generating millions of dollars per year and affording him and his family an enviable lifestyle. Can you imagine the joy, let alone the message of hope and perseverance, our society would have missed had Tyler Perry given up and given in. He made it through hard work, of course, but also through sheer will and a belief in his talent. Thankfully, there are others who did not give up either.

Cristiano Ronaldo

Cristiano Ronaldo may seem an unlikely person to include on this list. He is an internationally known sportsman, among the best-known and best-looking athletes on the planet. His annual salary exceeds $20 million, in addition to tens of millions more in endorsements. His net worth is hundreds of millions of dollars, a figure that allows Cristiano to buy mansions and a stable of cars that includes Lamborghinis and Rolls-Royces. He has become a certified legend in the field of soccer, collecting five Champion Trophies and a record-tying five Ballon d'Or awards, which is the annual football award presented to the sport's most valuable player (Ronaldo, 2018). Few have matched his athletic feats on the field, and even fewer have matched his commercial exploits off the field. He is one of the most marketable athletes on the planet.

Few remember how Cristiano's story began and what it took for him to get from a small country to international acclaim. He was born into a poor family, sharing a bedroom with his siblings, and left home at a young age to perfect his soccer skills at an academy in Lisbon, a traumatic event for some youth (Smith, 2017). Yet Cristiano was the first boy on the practice field, and he was among the last on his team to leave practice. That work ethic, combined with a talent and an almost unrivaled drive to reach his potential, made him not just a star, but an athlete and personality on a global scale.

Besides his work on the field, he has parlayed his wealth and success on the field into a devotion to charity. He is admired as much for his athletic prowess as for what he has done with the platform he has attained, which is to devote much of his time and some of his money toward helping the less fortunate.

Vincent Van Gogh

Vincent Van Gogh was one of the most brilliant painters in history, yet he incredibly only sold one painting in his lifetime. He made almost no money throughout his life, but he continued to paint because of the passion for his art and the belief in his work. Can you imagine working almost every day (in Van Gogh's case, painting more than nine hundred individual works of art) without ever enjoying the financial benefits of your time and effort (Van Gogh Gallery, 2018)? Van Gogh would spend days toiling over a canvas, transferring his visions and dreams into pictures that, at the time, few wanted or were willing to purchase. It must have been discouraging, disheartening, and depressing, but Van Gogh never quit.

Today, few of Van Gogh's painting come up for sale. Most of his paintings are in museums, from the Louvre to the Musée Rodin and the Rome Museum, mainly because few individuals can afford to purchase these paintings for their personal collections. Seldom does a Van Gogh painting go before the auction block, and those that do sell for tens of millions of dollars. In 1990, one of Van Gogh's paintings sold for more than $82 million, at the time the most expensive painting ever sold at auction (Winkel, 2014). Two of his most famous paintings, *The Starry Night* and *Sunflowers,* are at the Metropolitan Museum of Art, and each would sell for hundreds of millions, if they were ever sold. In fact, *The Starry Night* has been firmly ensconced as one of the ten most famous paintings to ever be completed, often rated second to the *Mona Lisa* in impact and popularity (Brushwiz, 2018; Halle, 2018; History Lists, 2018; Sawe, 2017). This picture, similar to the *Mona Lisa* by da Vinci, *The Girl with the Last Supper* by Vermeer, and *The Night Watch* by Rembrandt, are virtually priceless.

Van Gogh left his mark with his painting and through an inspiring work ethic and refusal to quit that has served as a model for almost any artist who has followed in his wake.

Theodor Geisel

Theodor Geisel, known professionally as Dr. Seuss, may be the most famous children's author in history. Selling more than six hundred million books, his books have been read billions of times, influencing generations of children and adults to read, think, dream, and have fun. Mr. Geisel published his first book, *And to Think That I Saw It on Mulberry Street,* in 1937, and the story of how that book was eventually published is quite interesting.

Mr. Geisel's first book was turned down twenty-seven times before a publisher decided to take a chance, and that chance arrived through a twist of fate. The man who eventually became Dr. Seuss was walking the streets of New York when he bumped into a friend from his alma mater, Dartmouth. Mr. Geisel mentioned that he was trying to sell a book that no one wanted to publish. His friend was recently hired as a junior editor at Vanguard Press, and their conversation happened to occur in front of the publishing headquarters where his friend worked. They walked inside, and as they say, the rest has become history (Gillett, 2016).

A slew of books eventually followed, including the classics *The Cat in the Hat, Green Eggs and Ham, How the Grinch Stole Christmas, and Oh the Places You'll Go* (Biography, 2018). These books are a staple of every library and any children's book collection, but dozens of publishers felt his writing lacked the literary and commercial appeal to publish the work. Can you imagine how devoid of imagination our childhoods would be had not one publisher decided to take a chance on Dr. Seuss?

Someone at Vanguard decided to take a chance on a story that no one thought would sell. Was Theodor Geisel a hard worker? Absolutely. Was he lucky? Maybe? Persistent? Most definitely. But he had a dream, and he was willing to make it come true no matter the obstacle.

It's not what we were given that is important—
but what we do with what we were given that matters.

Along with my maternal grandmother, my parents likewise preached the value of hard work all throughout their lives. Each had two jobs while they were young, and they raised four children. My father, a garbageman by day and a farmer by night, was a first-generation American. His parents both immigrated from Genoa, Italy. My mother, raised on welfare after her father abandoned his family for another woman, was a secretary by day and a telephone operator by night. My maternal grandmother helped in raising us children since my parents routinely worked ten- and twelve-hour days—and additional work on weekends. It was not an easy life, to be sure, but it became a great life.

My parents saved their money, invested in my father's garbage company and other real estate, and worked in that manner for almost four decades. In fact, long after they needed to work, they still worked. They say, "That's what we do … we're workers, and hopefully we contribute a little along the way as well." That philosophy has been instilled in my two brothers and sister. Each of us has had two jobs throughout most of our working years. We have also saved our money, invested in real estate and other business ventures, and contributed to society through public service and charitable donations.

We live in a land of unimagined opportunity, within a world of unlimited possibilities, at least for those who dream the impossible dream, are willing to work hard to achieve it, are kind to all they meet, and overcome any obstacles or criticism in their paths. Tyler Perry believed in his dream, Vincent Van Gogh believed in his talent, Dr. Seuss believed in his stories, and my parents believed in their work ethic. Through adversity and hardship, pain and peril, my parents and others like them made it because they believed in it, battled for it, sacrificed for it, and worked for it. In today's world of new industries and antiquated professions, working hard may not be the only path to professional security and stability, but few roads offer a better chance or a brighter promise than the ability and willingness to work hard.

Think Differently

The quest for immortality begins with curiosity.

We live in a world of differences, from varied religions to diverse races, and those differences consume the entirety of our existence. Few countries across the globe are inhabited by people of the same race or those born in the same country. Instead, there is broad diversity among people in nearly country that one may visit or inhabit. With the fall of dictators and oppressive ideological regimes, combined with the ease of transportation and search for greater economic opportunities, citizens are less willing and less likely to live their entire lives in the same country.

Today, France is less French, England is less English, and Germany is less German than at any time in memory. Approximately 10 percent of French citizens are foreign born, and in 2015, a record two million people immigrated to Germany, now calling that country their new home. These are seismic changes to a country that will change the language, customs, and cultures of their people. One nation, one language, and one culture no longer reflect the composition of many of the countries in this world, and the movement to more open borders, and have fewer restrictions on travel and immigration indicate that trend will continue.

Countries are becoming less isolated, both political and economically. On March 25, 1957, France, Italy, the Netherlands, Belgium, Luxembourg, and the country then known as West Germany (now known as Germany following the reunification of West and East Germany on October 3, 1990), signed the European Economic Community (History, 2018). That contract created what is known as the Common Market, to network of countries that sought to reduce trade barriers among the continental powers, and to encourage the exchange of goods and services between these countries with fewer restrictions. England joined the Common Market on January 1, 1973, after much fanfare and withstanding the previous objections of France, and was later joined by Ireland, Denmark, and Greece. As of 2018, there are twenty-eight countries throughout Europe that form the European Union, which became the successor to the original European Economic Community.

This new European Union advocates for closer communication and coordination between the member countries. The contract amount these countries goes far beyond trade and now encompasses advocating for a common defense and foreign policy, a single currency (for most countries in the European Union), and collaboration on environment, transport, and travel. In effect, each member country has surrendered much of its sovereignty to become a member state within a super state. France, Germany, and Italy, among other countries, are now one member of a common country called the European Union, similar, at least in some parts, to the states of California, Georgia, and Tennessee belonging to the United States. These European nations that once had their own language, customs, and cultures within its borders have fallen and, instead, represent a single member among a diverse people.

The United States, Canada, and Mexico have merged aspects of their economies through the North American Free Trade Act (NAFTA), which took force on January 1, 1994. Though not in scope or scale as the European Union—for example, each of the member countries retains its own foreign policy, defense, and currency—economic policy is more closely coordinated between the three countries. Since NAFTA's passage, trade barriers have fallen across much of North America, markets have opened to products previously barred through trade quotas and restrictions, customs procedures, and intellectual property rights, and investments between member countries have also been coordinated and codified (Office of the United States Trade Representative, 2018). Not all member countries have shared equally in its success—some believe NAFTA has been far more advantageous to Canada and Mexico than the United States—yet trade within all three countries has risen dramatically since its inception.

The Far East has been experiencing similar economic and political integrations, though on a smaller scale and at a slower pace. China is on the verge of becoming the most powerful country in the world, surpassing the United States. Some see China as the dominant country of the twenty-first century, following the dominance of the United States in the twentieth century. *The National* has even dubbed the twenty-first century as the "Eurasian century" (*The National, 2017)*. The emergence of China should have a domino effect on other countries within the Far East—from Singapore to Vietnam, Cambodia to South Korea—prompting an unprecedented growth in exports and incomes. Living standards are projected to skyrocket, enabling their populations to become more educated and more inventive. Along the way, their business acumen will become more pronounced, prompting countries in the Asian and Pacific Rim to become intertwined and integrated, creating joint ventures and collaborative partnerships that will bind these countries toward a more common purpose.

It is a circumstance that occurred with the European Union and the North America Free Trade Act, and it is a scenario envisioned with those nations in the Far East as well. Each of these blocks of countries, from Europe to North America and now to the Far East, has seen trade barriers reduced, imports and exports increased, and world markets opened to the country with the best product at the best price. The world's gross national product (GNP) has risen appreciatively as global competition and trade have expanded, though not equally and, according to some, fairly for every country within these trading blocks. More opportunities exist for barriers to free and fair competition to fall, including lower transportation costs and increased access to computers and telecommunications, at least for those countries and their competitors that create something different, something new, and something unique and for the countries and people who learn to think and act differently.

Different nations, different languages, and different cultures want products and services that cater to their unique backgrounds, desires, and hopes. They want something different, and they search for products and services that meet that need. Moreover, their needs are always changing, encouraged by their desire for something new and by a global competitive landscape that is now able to deliver something new, something different, and something cheaper. The competitive strength of an organization, similar to a country, does not last long, and the organization that hires those employees who can think different in order to make something different is the one that will live to work another day—if not another month or year.

The person who can think of a different and better future, believes it can happen, and then works to make it come true is the superstar every organization strives to acquire. This ability to think different and the capability to do something different is truly an ability within us all. Those who think and act differently—who use their hearts and minds to envision a different world—share four common traits and attributes: they are smarter and faster, they ask "what if" and "why not," they know they are right, and they are willing to at least try. Each is discussed in greater detail below.

Smarter and Faster

The right idea does not arise when someone is sleeping—and rarely when someone is playing. An idea arises when one studies what has worked in the past and what has not. A good idea arises when one learns about what organizations need and what customers want. A great idea arises when one uses what they studied and what they learned to create a different perspective and imagination, one founded on the knowledge of the mistakes of the past and the possibilities of the future.

The foundation of nearly any idea is education. Rare is the individual who envisions a product or service without extensive knowledge of that customer or industry. They know every aspect of that business, from how the product is made to what type of product a customer needs and wants. In fact, without that information, a person would have little knowledge on the type of good or service a customer is likely to purchase or how a product could be produced more efficiently. If a person does not possess or acquire this knowledge—gained through studious and continuous research—they would not know what is needed or wanted or maybe what is possible.

Steve Wozniak, Paul Allen, and Jeff Bezos offer a great illustration of the need and requirement to be smarter and faster than the competition. Each of these individuals identified something missing in their market and then had the knowledge, ambition, and determination to provide it. Steve Wozniak is an inventor who is often referred to as a genius; he produced the first computer with a typewriter-like keyboard (Rawlinson, 2017). He believed there should be a personal computer in every home, and he believed he and his friend Steve Jobs could make and sell this type of computer. Together, on April 1, 1976, they founded Apple Computers, which is among the most valuable businesses. Mr. Wozniak become one of the few who created that personal computer market, far surpassing even the most hopeful and futuristic of his ambitions.

Paul Allen believed in the power of the personal computer—but from a software framework. He researched software languages that powered computers and believed a more advanced program could be developed. Along with his partner, Bill Gates, that ambition eventually led to the creation of Microsoft, a firm that was soon to dominate the software that powers most computers. While Mr. Allen and Mr. Gates did not create the personal computer, their discovery served as the foundation for the explosive growth that occurred in the 1980s.

Finally, there is Jeff Bezos. Mr. Bezos believed the masses would buy their personal and business products online, and have them delivered to their door, if the right opportunity arose. For a lower price, and for the sake of convenience, if a business created this market, it could revolutionize the very manner in which people shopped for their goods and services. The then-requirement that products be purchased at the corner grocery market or storefront was soon to be outdated, or so Mr. Bezos believed, and the right business model could make that vision a reality. In 1995, Mr. Bezos launched Amazon, named after the largest river in the world, as a business that originally sold only books (Hartmans, 2017). Today, Amazon sells virtually any product manufactured or sold, has more than 310 million customers worldwide, employs 550,000 workers, and is the largest e-retailer in the United States (Cakebread, 2017; Statista, 2018). That company has made Mr. Bezos one of the most powerful, most influential, and richest business magnates on earth.

Each of these innovators knew their product and their audience, and they knew that their revolutionary idea would work. They could not wait. They were demanding, determined, and undeterred by any obstacles in their paths. They would be fast, and they would be first. Their ambitions started with the time and effort devoted to reading, studying, listening, researching, and experimenting, which are all fundamental to learning about what is missing and then knowing how a different tomorrow can be created.

Ask "What If?" and "Why Not?"

Rules, processes, and procedures were created to ensure that those who come after will follow the same path. The original path was shaped because it worked; thereafter, the organization created rules to ensure future employees followed that same path to achieve the same results. In the past, rules and processes were valued because the results were often preordained. There was a sense of consistency, even predictability, as long as an organization and its employees followed the rules and procedures. That, at least, was the theory, and it showed promise in a static environment.

However, there is no guarantee that the path will continue to work, especially since we live in a rapidly evolving environment that is continually changing the very nature in which organizations, employees, and customers operate. We live and work in anything other than a static environment. Science and technology have dramatically altered our national and international landscapes, and a host of variables—from tariffs to courts, taxes, to regulations—affect even the best designed and implemented strategies.

Of course, there is more risk in nearly any decision an organization and its employees undertake, which may deter some from taking a chance. This is one reason why rules and procedures offer so much solace to those in unpredictable environments. They believe it is safer to follow what has worked in the past and follow the rules created by those who came before. That, undoubtedly, will be a mistake of gigantean proportions for those in the workplace today. The environment upon which previous decisions and actions were taken no longer exists; the cultures, customs, and mores have changed. Therefore, the consequences of following the same path, time and time again, will doom an organization to complacency. Complacency, with little doubt, is the surest path to irrelevance for the organization that espouses that policy and an employee who follows that rule.

Rules and processes stop a person and an organization from thinking and asking the challenging questions such as "Can this be done better?" or "Why are we doing this at all?" Rules are another word for *no*; the preferred approach should be to question what has worked in the past to ensure environmental conditions are similar to what they were when the decisions were made. If those conditions change, then the decisions must change too—or at the very least be reexamined and reconsidered. That action, however, will not occur unless organizations encourage those questions to be asked and employees feel emboldened to challenge the status quo.

It is not easy to question authority. It takes courage, conviction, confidence, and surety in your actions. To think differently—to question the powerful and their decisions—one needs to first question the decisions that have been made, the path that is being taken, and the results that are desired. Then difficult and unpopular decisions need to be taken even if they are clouded in risk, if the road ahead has never been taken, and if the results are unforeseeable. These processes and decisions liberate one's thinking, casting aside the binds that force an organization to act and a person to think in a singular fashion.

Some years ago, the computer giant Hewlett-Packard produced a series of successful commercials where the employee, at the end of the commercial, asks, "What if?" Most of the commercial started with the announcer stating, "At HP, we're always thinking." This was followed by a number of scenarios where employees are performing seemingly routine and mundane tasks outside the workplace, all the while the employee is thinking about Hewlett-Packard and its customers. In one commercial, a Hewlett-Packard employee was showering at home and suddenly leaps from the shower, calls their coworker, and asks "What if?" In another popular commercial, a Hewlett-Packard employee is swimming laps in the pool while pondering a customer's problem. These commercials were produced to create the impression that if you do business with Hewlett-Packard, their employees will never stop thinking about how to make your business run better and be more profitable. These commercials were highly impactful and influential. They worked because they showed an overriding commitment by Hewlett-Packard and its employees toward the customer, creating and perpetuating an impression of Hewlett-Packard as innovative and forward-thinking.

Asking probing, even critical, questions can be threatening to some organizations and their employees. These questions are often asked of superiors who created the rules and processes that are followed, and some may interpret these questions as confrontational, disrespectful, divisive, or destructive to the organization. Some managers may be defensive of the past rather than prospective toward the future, and they may be distrustful of the messenger rather than grateful for the message. In both instances, it takes a brave and confident employee to question the status quo and believe there may be an alternative way that should be explored—or at least another path that should be considered and debated.

Asking these questions runs counter to our own upbringing. In our youth, we are taught to respect our elders and avoid questioning authority, whether it is our parents or teachers. They are the ones with the knowledge and experience, so we assume a learner attitude for most of our educational years, rarely venturing to assume the role of guide or teacher. This socialization runs into adulthood, which is where we become junior members of education (as freshmen in college) and then into organizations, where we become interns or trainees. Eventually, we become schooled to avoid confrontation, contention, and disagreements since they may affect our ability to obtain and maintain a job, a central pursuit during these ages.

Overall, we learn to "go along to get along," that collaboration is better than conviction, and that being a team player carries greater value than being the team leader. This can train, even force, us to listen rather than talk and follow rather than lead, both traits that suppress the mind from exceeding the confines of what we have been taught. The ones who rock the boat often become castigated, relegated to the back rather than appreciated because they have a different, and at times better, idea. In reality, the organizations that search for employees who "fit in" and are "team players" will be challenged in any knowledge-intensive, technology-laden, and fast-paced competitive market. Organizations that employ those who do not question, discuss, debate, and disagree about their futures can no longer expect to play constructive roles in their industries.

We have learned that the same product and service rarely exist for an extended period of time. Unless an organization is utilizing the creative insights of each employee, they will not develop a competitive advantage against others in the market. That rarely ends well. Moreover, the organization loses an important voice of constructive feedback and dissent who could right the ship before the organization embarks upon a path whose direction may be disadvantageous, even calamitous, to the organization and the employees who rely upon the organization for personal and professional advancement.

Among the most productive and profitable organizations are those that tolerate discussion, debate, and even dissent, albeit in a well-managed environment. Those organizations that allow—and even demand—disagreement and discord from those in their organizations create a culture of inquiry and innovation that generates more sound decisions and more deliberate actions. It falls to the organization to create this type of culture and the individual to become this type of employee. Employees must cast aside the shackles that bind their thinking and constrain their imaginations and relearn and reclaim that questioning spirit in a deliberate and respectful manner.

Employees who display the ability to ask the tough and probing questions—the "what ifs" and "why nots"—and then collaborate throughout the organization to determine the right answers help shape the direction of an organization and burnish their reputations as positive and constructive forces dedicated to advancing the interests of the organization. Applicants and employees with those traits are among the most sought out and valued, and they reinforce the importance of asking the right questions at the right time and then actively pursuing the right answers.

Believe in something good
and work to do something great.

Know They Are Right

Forces can confound and complicate the roads we travel. At times, this may cause some to unknowingly and unavoidably doubt their determination, distrust their abilities, and question their actions. There are simply too many we meet in our travels whose sole ambition is to impede our progress, mock our ambitions, and criticize our intentions, and the consequences of their actions can shake one's confidence and question one's resolve. At least, regrettably, for those without the confidence in their beliefs and the conviction in their dream.

By contrast, those persons and employees who are among the most treasured are those who believe in something good and work to achieve something great. Moreover, they have an unshakable belief in what they know, where they are going, and how they are going to get there. They know they are right, and with that assurance, they embark upon exploration into the unknown—with the realization that the voyage is worth the adventure and the rewards are worth the risk.

This type of confidence is unique to an individual. The past is replete with more reasons why something will not work than why it might work and where someone failed rather than succeeded. Yet history recalls those few visionaries who moved the world in a different direction and celebrates those few achievements that changed the face—for the better—of the world in which we live.

Whether it is the camera or cell phone, printing press or internet, light bulb or artificial heart, those who persevered against perceived insurmountable odds did so because they had an unquestionable belief in their idea, an unassailable confidence in their ambition, regardless of the obstacle or barrier, danger or peril, criticism or adversity.

Unflappable against danger and unflustered against obstruction, these few individuals became unstoppable toward triumph. This is a trait shared by those who are achievers and is a characteristic of those who are accomplished. Employees and applicants who possess this trait are cherished and prized in the workplace. They believe a different way might be a better way. Through education, experience, research, experimentation, and hard work, employees who develop the unassailable belief that they know they are right—no matter the circumstances unforeseen and consequences realized—offer organizations a person of unique drive and ambition, and this person can be the differentiating factor between failure and success.

Ideas do count,
and results do matter,
but first you have to try.

At Least Try

Ideas do count, and results do matter. Thankfully, the world is inhabited by many with wonderous ideas; sadly, the world is inhabited by too few who turn their ideas into reality. The advances in computers, telecommunication, transportation, and media have transformed our world from the idea of something different and from the effort to do something different. Someone did something with what they dreamed and what they had—or at least they tried. They tried to make their dreams come true, tried to reach their potential, and tried to realize their ambitions.

Not every sixth grader scores an A in English, and not every seventh grader scores an A in math. Not every prospective college student scores a perfect score on their Scholastic Aptitude Test or is accepted by every college of their choice. Not every applicant for a job is hired, and not every employee is promoted to the job of their dreams. But at each stage of one's life, a person can at least try and take a chance. This is a trait employers are looking for in an employee: someone with the dream and the will to achieve it.

In this universe, there are too many variables that disrupt the best-designed plans and too few assurances that guarantee success to judge one's accomplishments on results alone. It is unfair and unrealistic. A farmer can toil from morning to night, tilling their land and planting the perfect row of tomatoes or wheat, yet a sudden change in the weather can destroy their crops before they can be harvested. A talented chef can compile the most amazing ingredients and create the most spectacular foods, yet their restaurant may open before a severe recession. An author may write the great American play, find the greatest director of the generation, and hire the most talented actor in memory, yet a biased and unfair review of the play may seal its fate. Finally, an applicant may be the most qualified for the position but miss an interview because of a mechanical breakdown of their automobile or be in the unfortunate circumstance of applying for a position against another candidate related to, or well known by, influential people in the organization and therefore preselected for the position. In this case, the application process was only a formality. These individuals may have worked hard and been supremely qualified and talented, yet success eluded them. Success may have been taken from them—against their will and against what is right—but success cannot take away the effort. At least they tried against often unprecedented opposition and unquestioned unfairness.

The ability to think something different is a unique characteristic, and the willingness to do something different is a unique trait. The person who offers both to an employer can become a superstar with unequaled rivals, the type of person who views failure as a brief delay before inevitable success. Be *that* person—the one who tries no matter the odds of success or likelihood of failure, who keeps trying no matter what end is realized—and you can better choose what you do and where you go. In a world of unpredictability, few have that luxury, but more could if only they would at least try.

In summary, the willingness and ability to think differently is reflective of those who are smarter and faster than others, who question what "is," who ask "what if" and "why not," who know beyond reason or doubt that they are right, and who at least try to do something grand and great. These individuals are unique in the workplace and become a commanding presence in whatever organizations they join. If you have the talent and determination to think differently, your path will be different. It will be punctuated with promise, not peril, and pride, not regret.

What matters is not whether we achieved our hopes or realized our dreams;
what matters is whether we tried:

tried to make someone better,
tried to make something better,
tried to be good,
and tried to do good.

Adapt and Adjust

We have learned that, in 2016, the average employee has been in their current job 4.2 years (down from 4.6 years in 2014) and will have between twelve and fifteen different jobs by the age of forty (Doyle, 2018). We have seen that, in the 1920s, the average life span of those companies listed in S&P 500 was sixty-seven years; by 2012, the average life span of those companies listed in the S&P 500 was only fifteen years (Gittleson, 2012). Finally, we have heard from an influential study by scientists at the Santa Fe Institute in New Mexico published in the *Royal Science Interface* that the average company ceases to exist after ten years, either through acquisitions, mergers, bankruptcy, or other reasons (Ivengar, 2015). These trends are troubling, worrisome, and even disheartening, and the conclusions are unmistakable: jobs are vanishing, organizations are fading at an alarming rate, and employees are transitioning from organization to organization at a much greater pace than in previous generations.

Instability is not limited to organizations and their employees. Political systems and societal relationships do not last to the same degree as in previous centuries. The systems and relationships that are among the most stable are those where citizens enjoy economic freedom and monetary independence. A sound financial structure that provides promising employment opportunities at a fair and decent wage is the lynchpin for nearly any political system or societal relationship—or at least one that expects to maintain the respect and reverence within its sphere. Creating and maintaining that financial structure and social fabric is a complex and controversial endeavor, which few countries in our age have conquered, and it is a principle factor in the rise of instability among the populace.

Political systems and societal relationships and organizations and employees share one ambition: to adapt and adjust to a rapidly changing world, including the economy, political institutions, and society. Very little, if anything, lasts for long anymore, at least in its current configuration. Those who have the best chance of lasting are those who have learned the art of adapting and the skill of adjusting, a trait the most secure applicants and employees of today have acquired. They have done so because they have learned from history, learned something new, and learned to take risks. Each of these aspects are expanded upon below.

Learn from History

Nicholas Clairmont wrote an article that included the famous phrase: "Those who do not learn history are doomed to repeat it." That may not be absolutely true, but as Mark Twain once famously said, "History does not repeat itself, but it does rhyme" (Clairmont, n.d.). There are numerous examples of leaders of countries and of industry who embark upon ventures that failed in the past yet believe different times will produce different outcomes. Napoleon believed France had the military prowess to conquer Russia. Unfortunately for his country—and fortunately for the world—he timed the invasion to occur during the harshest part of the Russian winter. His army was decimated, in part, by the weather. More than a century later, Germany believed they could conquer Russia as part of their World War II campaign. More than thirty million men and women lost their lives during this campaign, which resulted in Germany's loss partly from the same brutal Russian winter that stymied Napoleon. Thankfully, each encountered the same fate: the lesson from history was not learned, and the same outcome was realized. Tragedy is not an isolated circumstance since the same circumstances often produce the same results.

History records the successes and failures of the past, and those who research these histories become more knowledgeable about what worked and did not work and why failure occurred and success was evaded. In each case, the ability to research, investigate, analyze, and interpret the past can be a determining factor in achieving something different. The same circumstances produce the same outcomes; different circumstances have a chance to produce different outcomes. In reality, yesterdays are only important if you can use these lessons to create a different tomorrow and create different circumstances that lead to a different future.

Among the most cherished traits of an employee or applicant are those who possess a solid educational foundation along with the depth and breadth of experiences as to when, how, and where strategies should be enacted and actions should be taken. Without education, an employee has little knowledge to rely upon in a given situation; without experience, an employee has little wisdom to utilize in a given opportunity. Those who possess of the most comprehensive of educations and broadest of experiences develop a keen insight into the mistakes of the past and the lessons that can be learned. We may live in a world where differences are valued over sameness and where unique is preferred over commonality, but there remains much we can learn from the past if we explore its lessons. These lessons become the knowledge utilized to create something—and in some cases anything—different so that those mistakes are not repeated.

You cannot do what is possible—
unless you can see what is possible.

Learn Something New

If we read the same books, talk to the same people, and travel the same roads, we will read the same words, talk the same thoughts, and see the same sights. We learn the same plots and storylines, hear the same stories and philosophies, and see the same museums and palaces. With few exceptions, there is little excitement in reading the same book, talking to the same person, and seeing the same site time and time again. Moreover, very little in our minds will change from our thoughts, perspectives, and beliefs, and very little will deviate from our actions, aspirations, and ambitions. What we have been is what we will continue to be, principally because our minds, hearts, and souls are devoid of possibilities, the possibilities of doing something different because we have learned something different.

When we do something different, we have the opportunity to think something different or be something different. Reading a new book can illuminate a state-of-the-art theory or process; talking with a new acquaintance can unearth a unique perspective or uncommon conviction; traveling to new lands can expose an unexplored civilization or unknown culture. Learning a foreign language, cultivating a new friendship, playing a new instrument, and joining a new club all have the potential to mold the philosophy and character of an individual. One becomes, in many respects and to a large extent, what one is exposed to, and the broader the spectrum one is exposed to, the greater the opportunity one has to become and be different.

For many, we live lives of habit. Our time is consumed with what we know, and we have determined what we like. We have determined that simplicity and tradition are comforting and reassuring, and we grow to appreciate the routines that pervade our lives. We enjoy running and have little desire to learn boxing; we already have friends and too little time to meet new acquaintances; we have a job and therefore make scant effort to find a new one or a better one. We have also seen that the same roads result in the same destination, sameness is not valued in the products we consume or the applicants we hire, and differences have become the rule rather than the exception. If you want a different job, or a better job, you must become different and better yourself, which means adapting to a new present and adjusting to a new future. That comes in a large part and to a large degree by learning something new.

Without education, one lacks the foundation to know what to do; without experience, one lacks the wisdom to know how to do it.

Learn to Take Risks

By learning something new or different, by expanding upon what we know or believe, we become aware of the possibilities that exist. Through research and development, an organization might become aware of a product that could revolutionize the industry; through innovation and exploration, an employee might develop a new service that could transform a market. The possibilities may exist, but you must do something with what you know and act upon what you have learned. Being aware of what is possible provides the idea or lesson; taking the opportunity to pursue what is possible takes initiative, courage, will, perseverance, and fortitude. It demands the ability and willingness to take calculated risks.

Risks can be calculated through research, analysis, and experiment. A proposed new product might have a 20 percent chance of success, or a new service might have a 60 percent chance of failure. The amounts and types of rewards are often determined by the surety and levels of risk; the lower the risk, the lower the rewards, and the greater the risk, the greater the rewards. To have the opportunity to gain all, one must take the opportunity to risk all, a scenario foreign to those who have learned that evolutionary advances are preferred to revolutionary zeal, and for those who are certain that pedestrian approaches are favored to seismic restructurings.

Today's customers seek something new and demand something innovative; both require an organization and its employees to create something that does not exist and embark upon a concept that may not become a reality. Those who assume this risk to create something new and innovative—and create a market that does not exist yet—have an opportunity to become pioneers in their fields. Think about Alexander Graham Bell and the telephone, Walt Disney and animation, or Mozart and musical composition. They saw the possibility, believed in their talent, and assumed the risk no matter if the result was success or failure, renown or ridicule.

How does one know when to take risk and when to avoid it? How does an employee know when to risk their reputation or their future? That may be an unanswerable question since there are so many variables that complicate the calculation of risk. For instance, one cannot predict with absolute certainty how a person or the public will react in a given situation until the situation presents itself. An applicant cannot learn with complete confidence what an organization is seeking from a prospective employee until the applicant enters the interview process, and an employee cannot understand the level of risk an organization is willing to tolerate on a venture until success or failure is realized. However, an individual should consider several questions when determining the level of risk:

- What is the chance of success? Risk can be calculated, but uncertainty cannot be calculated. If you can reasonably calculate the chance of success (for instance, there is a 55 percent chance of success), you have the knowledge to make a more informed decision.
- Can you afford the failure? Will your reputation withstand any damage that may arise from a failure? An actor who has enjoyed four or five consecutive commercial successes can afford a commercial failure, but a rising actor's career may not weather an early commercial failure. Similarly, a new manager may not overcome an early mistake or miscalculation. In both instances, the actor and the manager may play it safe until they develop a history and reputation that may withstand a mistake or a disappointment.
- Do you have a plan B? As mentioned earlier, the greater the risk, the greater the reward—but also the greater the chance of failure. The risk is more palatable if a person has something to fall back on. If a person has the financial resources to withstand a loss, the ability to return to a previous job if one is lost, or others to rely upon in the event of a failure, one may be more willing to assume the risk.

There are few rewards without risks, and the greater the risk, the greater the possibility of both success and failure. Many know what is possible, but few are willing to do what is possible, and the few who do are among the most cherished in an economy and marketplace that values the ability to think—and be—different. The historical figures of our age did something with what they were given, often regardless and irrespective of the risks. Those who adopt this ambition become the singular influencers of their day because the likelihood of success or failure is often secondary to the belief in their cause and pursuit of their passion—and because they are willing to take a chance.

In times of great instability and tremendous uncertainty, those who display an ability and willingness to adapt to a different future become among the most appreciated in an organization. The superstars of today have a talent that is uncommon, an idea that is unrivaled, a confidence that is unshakable, and a determination that is unwavering. They have learned from history about what was possible and impossible, and they sought to learn something new in the hopes of creating something different. When they found that idea, they took a risk because it might work. These attributes are common to the ambitious and uncompromising, and they are uncommon to the average and undecided. Most importantly, these are the characteristics of those who do not merely adapt and adjust to a changing world. They create a future that others must adapt and adjust to. They control their own destinies and determine their own fates, a rare circumstance for employees in today's globally competitive environment.

We must adapt to an unknown and unexpected future,
one where ambiguity is present and certainty is suspect.

Be Loyal and Caring

Loyalty is a word one hears infrequently in the workplace today. The average tenure of an employee continues to decrease, and there are few instances of employees remaining with the same employers for twenty or thirty years, let alone ten years. The customer is too fickle, and competition too fierce, for organizations to offer employees any semblance of long-term employment. That realization has led employees to be more amenable to accepting employment in other organizations, often in the hope of finding a more stable organization with a more promising future. Consequently, employees are less committed in their organizations, and organizations are less invested in their employees.

Loyalty, to a large extent, no longer exists. It has become a more transitory workplace, which some would say mirrors the transitory nature of society. From friendships to marriages, automobiles to jobs, not much seems to last anymore. The success of today is the failure of tomorrow, and the wealth gained in one year is lost in the next. It is a turbulent world, one marked by a certain coldness and heartlessness between organizations and its employees, and between friends and acquaintances. Against this backdrop is the kind and gentle soul, a person who displays the best of humility in themselves and conveys the best of humanity in others. They think the best, believe the best, act the best, and wish the best to all within their path, and anyone within earshot of a caring word and a kind deed.

In an era where there may be slivers of dissimilarity between knowledge, skills, and abilities—where the slightest advantage can result in the greatest difference—an applicant who displays kindness toward others may be the discerning factor between one who is hired and one who is not, one who is promoted or demoted, retained or dismissed. In the workplaces I have either worked in or consulted with, those employees seen as the kindest and most generous almost always secure positions somewhere in the organization, often in positions above what their skills and abilities would support. That is the attraction, and power, of a kind disposition in the workplace.

The workplace is too competitive, and the differences among applicants and employees are too minute, to discount the value of an applicant or employee who displays a caring attitude toward others, in addition to a loyal and dedicated observance of the organization's purpose and mission. Such individuals have two attributes—a belief in others and a belief in the cause—that display a care and humanity toward others, and an allegiance and faithfulness toward an organization, which have been indispensable to the triumphant applicant and champion employee.

Believe in Others

Organizations are created because the efforts of one person are insufficient for accomplishing an objective. It takes the collaborative efforts of many individuals, and numerous departments, performing their assigned duties and tasks in an efficient and effective manner, for organizations to have a chance at success. At the heart of this ambition is an individual's willingness and ability to subordinate their own interests to the collective gain of the organization. In times where organizations are not always able to reward employees for their service, let alone their sacrifice, this type of attitude and ethic is solely missed in the workplace.

Yet it is this type of person who is highly sought, and treasured, because of their impact on the organization and its members. A person who strives to create relationships among coworkers, encourages others to reach their potential, and offers a helping hand to those in need can have a weighty and positive influence on the organization. These types of employees retain roles in the organization often beyond their capabilities, and they are often among the last to be dismissed in challenging times. They are selfless and giving, and in the process, they help create an inclusive and supportive culture that inspires other employees to reach for the impossible—and some nearly attain it.

In an age where loyalty to an organization is rare, and personal sacrifice to the greater good is even more rare, employees who display this type of disposition can obtain and retain a unique status in an organization. Employees are drawn to coworkers who think more of others than they often do of themselves, supervisors are drawn to subordinates who help others achieve their ambitions before they achieve their own, and organizations are drawn to employees who place the success of the organization before the promotion of their own interests. Coworkers, supervisors, and organizations respect and admire these individuals, endeavoring to work with those who display a basic sense of goodness and giving throughout all their interactions. They have faith in this type of person, the faith that they will comport themselves in an unselfish, fair, just, and honorable manner that benefits all rather than some and the organization rather than the individual.

To some, we live in a world where a sense of goodness may be uncommon and a belief in giving may be infrequent. To others, we live in a world where helping others—whether they are the less fortunate or the most fortunate—reflects a society confident in their values, appreciative of their circumstances, and optimistic for the future. We have apathy for the former, and faith in the latter. Those who uphold the values of goodness and giving are the first hired in good times and the last fired in challenging times, and they embody what others hope to emulate: a good person trying to do good things. Find that type of person in your organization, and be that type of person for your employer, and you can obtain a sense of personal and professional stability virtually unknown in today's world: a good person trying to do good things.

Believe in the Cause

Among the most committed and loyal employees are those who have an unwavering belief in the products their organizations produce and the services they create. Find an employee who is passionate about where they work and what they make, and you will find an employee who is passionate about what they do. That is the type of applicant organizations seek to employ, and the type of employee that employers seek to retain, because their actions are supported by an utter belief in the purpose and ambitions of the organization. There are those who join the military to safeguard their country's citizens or become police officers to help create a civil society. Some seek to create a business to provide employment opportunities for at-risk youth or deliver services to those confined in their homes. Still others may become teachers to educate the next generation of adults to become respectful and contributing members of society or become construction workers to build the roads and bridges upon which we all travel. All are admirable and worthy causes; organizations that match the right employee with the right type of work can achieve nearly any ambition.

As an employer, how do you attract and retain the most committed and loyal employees? The characteristics of the organizations that employees most want to work for center around four characteristics: treating is employees fairly, putting employees first, offering a stable and promising future, and creating interesting and valued work.

Treating Employees Fairly

Good organizations hire, compensate, and promote employees based on their abilities, and they do so in a fair and just manner. There is no favoritism showed to some or bias shown to others. Instead, employees are judged by their contributions and accomplishments, and they share in the rewards of organizational success to an extent that's generally viewed as fair.

Putting Employees First

Few employees seek an employer who takes advantage of their work, neglects their interests, or makes them feel insignificant. Employees search for employers who create a workplace with the greatest opportunity to be healthy, happy, and hopeful. These employers truly care about the interests and ambitions of their employees and craft strategies that fulfill the hearts and souls of those who devote their time and efforts to ultimately benefit the organization. Good organizations create an employee-friendly workplace, where telecommuting and flexible schedules are available where appropriate, where employees can utilize their ingenuity and discretion in their jobs, where rewards are shared and achievements are celebrated as a team, where the needs of the employee are as important as the needs of the organization, and where managers treat everyone with respect and coworkers treat each other with kindness.

Almost nothing matches the degree of satisfaction an employee will gain and the performance an employee will give to an organization or another person when they feel that organization or that person cares about them and their well-being. Find that type of organization as an employee, and create that type of organization as an employer, and nearly any mission or vision has a chance to be realized.

Offering a Stable and Promising Future

One of the most difficult commitments an employer can offer an employee is that they will have a job as long as they work hard and commit to the organization. No matter the effort extended, or the promise seen, the world is too unstable in terms of technology, computerization, and consumer preferences for organizations to offer any semblance of possibilities to their employees. However, organizations can effectively manage their operations, invest in their future, and build their workforce to better place themselves to take advantage of whatever eventuality may come their way.

The key is *possibilities*. Employees want to work for organizations where there is a possibility of success and believe that it can be achieved, sustained, and continued. Creating such an organization enhances the commitment of the best employees to remain with the organization, even during the short-term challenges that are inevitable in any business cycle. However, those organizations most adept at meeting the challenges of the present and creating opportunities for the future can offer a stable, bright tomorrow, which that can result in a more dedicated and committed workforce.

We hope to live in a world where the struggling are given hope and the ambitious are given promise.

Creating Interesting and Valued Work

Most employees want to feel that they have done something and accomplished something of value in their lifetimes. Organizations that can create work that satisfies the basic instinct of a person to matter can greatly enhance the motivation of an employee to do their job and the commitment of an employee to stay in that job. Some jobs do not lead themselves to meaningful work, at least on the surface, but almost any job satisfies some need of the public or meets some desire of another.

The duty of an organization and its managers is to convey how the accomplishment of a job, and of the organization's mission, will satisfy the needs, hopes, and desires of the public. This could be the supermarket that provides food to society or the carpenter who provides housing for a community. Those who struggle to identify the societal benefit of their organization can still allocate a portion of their profits to help a charity or nonprofit so that the organization and its members will feel a sense of pride and worth in what they do. They can see that the fruits of their efforts are going—at least in part—to benefit those who may be less fortunate than others. This can satisfy a basic need of individuals and employees to feel that they are contributing to the advancement of humankind. It is a powerful motivation for some to work harder, and to commit longer, to the positions they hold and the organizations they work for.

That is how an employer can attract and retain the most committed and loyal of employees. Conversely, how does an employee know the type of work that will lead them to be among the most committed and loyal of employees—or even like their job? They find this work through three pursuits: following their passion, finding the fun along the way, and searching for meaning in what they do.

Passion

Passion is the intense desire that consumes your mind, heart, and soul. Everyone has a passion for someone and a desire for something. Few may devote their lives to following that passion, but it remains the unbridled love of their life. There are those who abandon all reason and logic to pursue their passion to be a professional tennis player or a United States senator even though both ambitions may be beyond their capabilities. Regardless, their passion overrules the mind and fills the heart, and throughout the journey, they are following what they love.

For the confident and courageous seeking to follow the passion of their lives, the reward lies not in the end but in the journey. The utter excitement and thrill that arises from following that which is loved can rarely be replicated in any other position or organization. A person who finds a profession that strokes their passion may not leave that particular job, profession, or industry. Likewise, employers that create jobs that employees become passionate about—that speak to their hearts, stimulate their minds, and stir their souls—may have employees for the indefinite future.

Fun

After an organization meets an employee's basic necessities—fair pay, medical benefits, some semblance of security and stability—employees search for an industry and profession that stirs their passions. If a person is courageous enough, and fortunate enough, to achieve those ambitions, then they look for organizations that offer them the best opportunities to enjoy their time and their lives.

Given the choice between working in a factory or riding an amusement ride, most would choose the amusement ride. Given the choice between eating broccoli or a candy bar, most would choose a candy bar. In 2018, our family traveled to Europe on our annual summer vacation. In Finland, my daughter (Tori) and my niece and nephew (Dalton and Bailey) chose to visit an amusement park rather than visit the historical sites of Helsinki. In Saint Petersburg, they chose to play golf rather than visit Catherine's Palace, one of the great wonders of that country. That is the attraction and intrigue of something that is fun.

If an employee found a job where their enjoyment was similar to riding an amusement ride or eating a candy bar, it would be a rarity for that employee to pursue other opportunities. Applicants want to find employers where they can have fun, and employees want to remain with an employer where they work among friends. We spend time doing things that bring enjoyment to our lives, and we do them better—both in terms of performance and productivity—when we like what we are doing.

Fun and friends remain at the heart of those ambitions and are powerful enticements to keep doing the same thing, at the same place, for the same people. Create that type of organization, and if an applicant finds that type of employer, the organization will have an employee for many years to come. Employees who like what they do, where they work, who they work for, and who they work with rarely pursue other opportunities. In regard to what they do, that starts with a passion for what the industry and profession does. Once employees determine and follow their passions, it becomes a matter of where they work, who they work for, and who they work with.

Meaning

From the founding of the United States up until the mid-1900s, most sought employment to purchase the necessities of life. Few viewed their jobs as mechanisms for fulfilling their inner demands and desires. In fact, many followed the jobs of their fathers; sons of a carpenter became carpenters, and sons of factory workers became factory workers. This became more common because few sons left the areas where they were born. Most were born and died in the same general area, mainly because travel was particularly expensive and uncommon during much of this time.

Conversely, women mainly worked in the home, taking care of their children and extended families, work that was made more difficult because of the extraordinary time that managing a household consumed, from cooking meals to washing clothes and cleaning house. By the 1950s, the growing dominance of the United States in the world markets meant many more jobs were available to men to pursue, and by the 1960s, opportunities for women became more pronounced. Moreover, the prevalence of travel allowed many more to travel freely across the world, and economic stability (mainly from the success of those born after World War II) meant the generation raised in the 1960s could attend college, broadening their awareness of what could be pursued and their aspirations of what was possible.

These opportunities allowed participants to be more selective in what they do and search for positions that offered more than a salary. They sought positions that offered *meaning*. As a result, men and women were able to think more broadly, even philosophically, about what they really wanted to do and who they really wanted to be. Most individuals, as they enter the final years of their lives, hope to look back upon their time on earth and feel that their lives mattered, that what they did and what they contributed mattered to more than their families. They may, in the dawn of life, strive to make a living, but in the twilight of life, they strive to make a difference. They want to create a business that provides others with a place to work, a charity that provides the less fortunate with a place to eat, a park that provides children with a place to play, or a senior center that provides the elderly with a place to converse with others.

Most yearn for the opportunity to do something worthwhile, mainly because it allows them to be someone admirable. More than any other factor—money, position, or title—the ability of an organization to provide, and employees to find, a job that allows employees to feel a sense of pride, honor, and meaning in what they do will create a sense of loyalty between the organization and its employees that rarely will waver.

Employers and organizations seek applicants who are loyal and caring. They want to hire, train, and develop a person who remains faithful, true, and determined to remain at the organization. Relationships form the bedrock between organizations and their customers, and the same remains true between organizations and their employees. A caring disposition, and a loyal person, serve as traits among the most admired employees because they display a belief in others and a commitment to others that create a sense of shared sacrifice and collective advancement for those within the organization. In a transitory world where foundations are unsteady and futures unsure, these are desirable attributes for almost any applicant seeking a job or any employee seeking continued employment.

Summary

The competition to become and remain employed has rarely been so fierce, and the job opportunities in the coming years remain daunting for those seeking a job, let alone the good job. Those best positioned to be employed have a set of skills and characteristics perfectly attuned to a workplace demanding a level of knowledge and competence that is constantly shifting changing. The best employees of today have the ability and willingness to work hard, mainly because very little is accomplished or achieved without hard work. Search far and wide, and in almost every instance, those who achieve the most have worked the most.

The second characteristic of the best employees are those who can think differently. Few organizations and their customers want something similar; instead, they demand something better. Employees who offer their organizations better do so because they are smarter and faster than others. In their search for something new, they constantly ask, "What if?" and "Why not?" They know they are right, and they are not afraid to try to achieve the most intimidating ambitions. If you can think different, you have an opportunity to be different, and if you can be different, you have a chance to create something different, a defining characteristic of the most innovative and imaginative minds and hearts.

The third characteristic of the right employee is the ability to adapt and adjust to an unknown and unexpected future—one where ambiguity is present and certainty is suspect. The most adaptable employees have learned from the misses and mistakes of history, learned something new that broadened their minds and hearts, and learned to take risks by appreciating success and accepting failure. Employees with this characteristic are uniquely positioned to contribute to the success of nearly any global organization.

The final characteristic of the right employee is a sense of loyalty to the cause and to others. The life span of an organization may be far shorter than at other time in history, and employees may have

far more jobs in their working lives than previous generations, yet organizations still value the dedication and commitment of their most ardent supporters and contributors. Organizations, employees, and customers continue to value the generosity of spirit and purity of heart that comes for those who care about others. Become the type of person and employee who is loyal and caring, works hard, thinks differently, and adapts to a changing world, and a relationship can be created between an employee and the organization that will withstand the tremendous pressures and anxieties of today's workplaces.

Those who live their own lives,
dream their own dreams,
develop their own talents,
and follow their own ambitions …
those who fight the good fight,
do the right thing at the right time and for the right reason,
and make the most of the road they travel,
are the ones the stars shine the brightest upon.

4

BECOMING THE RIGHT PERSON

*If you want to work at the right organization,
if you want to be the right employee,
you first must become the right person.*

Most aspire to find the perfect job with the perfect organization, and for a time, some realize their ambition. But that quest, and subsequent conquest, will be a fleeting triumph unless one becomes a person who is unfailingly kind and caring, admirable and honorable, and good and decent. These are the type of employees who recruiters want to meet, supervisors want to hire, customers want to do business with, coworkers want to work with, and friends want to spend time with. The fortunate and determined who become this type of person, who become this type of human being, is bestowed with untold financial rewards and incalculable personal accolades that represent a person of character and congeniality. This person is not just the right person for the job—but the right person for the world.

But how does one become that type of individual: a good employee and a good friend, a good coworker and a good person? Becoming a good person, and becoming the right person, takes a person of character and conviction, of will and perseverance. It takes a person who lives in a way that demands admiration, commands respect, and inspires others to emulate their lives. These individuals are certainly unique and uncommon, yet the attributes they possess are common and attainable to all.

The six traits that are most characteristic of this type of person—who chooses to follow the right path, decides to make the right decision, and fights to chase the right dream—are presented below and incorporated into the acronym BOATES, a word that represents adventure, wonderment, serenity, and tranquility. Those who seek what is good and pursue what is honorable live a life of adventure and wonderment and serenity and tranquility, knowing they are doing the doing the right thing with the hopes of becoming the right person. The six traits are:

- doing the *best* with what they have
- having *options* in life—because nothing lasts
- *always* looking for the good along the road of life
- remembering *they* have to live that life
- being *extraordinarily* kind
- going down *swinging* for who they are and what they stand for

Do the Best with What You Have

> *The accomplished, the admired, and the honored*
> *are those who did something with what they had.*

In many ways, life is like a deck of playing cards. Every deck has cards, but no two players get the exact same cards from the deck. Two persons may each receive a straight flush or four of a kind, but they can never obtain the same straight in the same suit or the same four cards in a deck. Some may obtain a great playing hand, seemingly hand after hand, while others may seemingly receive poor playing hands. At first, some may believe the hand they received is the result of luck, and that may be true over a brief period of time. However, over a longer period, we realize that other factors determine your overall success in cards; luck is only one factor. One can learn to study the game, devote oneself to learning the intricacies of each game, and practice relentlessly over time. While one can never escape luck, over time, luck becomes only one factor among the many that determine the eventual success or failure of the card player.

Several lessons we learn from playing cards are applicable to the workplace as well. First are odds. It is true that odds play a role in the success of a card player. For instance, according to Poker Hand Probability (2018), there are more than 2.5 million possible hands from a single deck. A player may be the one player in every 64,974 hands who receives a straight flush or the one player in every 694 hands who receives a full house. More likely, a player is only one in every 2.3 hands who is dealt a pair. Success in cards can be calculated, and over time, we learn that the odds balance out. Someone who plays long enough eventually will be dealt a straight flush, and more often than not, they will receive a pair.

Another lesson learned from playing cards, similar to the workplace, is the importance of skill, decision-making, and temperament, which often have a greater influence on your success than odds. Professional card players study the odds (using their education), determine when to fold their hands or double down (using their experience), and play over a longer period of time so the odds become more balanced (using their perseverance). They also learn when to control their emotions so that others do not see their excitement when they are dealt an amazing hand or their dejection when the cards received are less than desired. Education, experience, and skill may not play a role in the specific cards you are dealt, but they play a specific role in how you *play* the cards you are dealt.

Here is a final lesson from playing cards. It is often how you respond to events—some beyond your control—that determines your eventual success. How one responds to the circumstances they encounter often determines their success, far more than any specific card or situation that has been dealt. Some confront the circumstances they face and strive to overcome the challenges in their path; others search for someone to blame and evade responsibility to take control over their future. While odds may play a role in the circumstances you encounter, they do not determine your success. Instead, it is how you respond to the circumstances you confront—in effect, how you play the cards you were dealt at that point in time—that determines any success you might encounter. In the end, you must do the best you have with what you have been given.

Kings have their palaces, presidents have their glory, movie stars have their worldwide fame, and the wealthy have their fortunes, but behind every façade lies a heartbreak, a loss, or a regret. Few leave this world without encountering a devastating failure, a relationship ending unexpectedly, a friend gone too soon, or an opportunity wasted foolishly. Ronald Reagan became the president of the United States yet suffered with Alzheimer's in his later years. J. Paul Getty was once the richest man in the world, yet his children battled adultery, drugs, suicide, and a kidnapping. Heath Ledger, Judy Garland, Prince, and Philip Seymour Hoffman are among the most revered actors of their generations, with each winning Academy Awards, yet they all succumbed to the ravages of drugs or alcohol.

If there is one maxim in life, it is that no one has it all. No one is the most beautiful, the most wealthy, the most loved, the most respected, or the most brilliant. No one has attained the happiest attitude, created the perfect children, and lived a faultless life. And no one has found the perfect job. There is a level of dejection, disappointment, regret, and unhappiness in everyone we meet. The only difference is that some focus on their disappointments, and others do not. We cannot determine the cards we have been dealt, but we can determine how we play them.

The content, the hopeful, and the happy are those who make the most of what they have, regardless of the criticism and adversity they encounter. There are challenges that consume one's present and obstacles that foreshadow their future, but they become barriers only when one does not have the will or fortitude to overcome them. Fame, fortune, intelligence, talent, health, and beauty are not distributed equally, but they are distributed fairly. Some achieve fame and others fortune, some possess intelligence and others talent, some are healthy and others beautiful, and while no one has it all, everyone has something.

From Mark Twain to Mark Wahlberg, Mark Zuckerberg to Pope Mark, Aaron Burr to Elvis Aaron Presley, and Roger Staubach to Roger Federer, each were given a trait, a characteristic, a talent that no one else has. We know of their astounding gift because they did something with it, something that gained them fame or fortune. Aaron Burr's success in the Revolutionary War eventually led him to politics and his election to vice president of the United States. Elvis Presley used his amazing tone and gift of song to become the preeminent and most successful singer of the twentieth century. But we know little of the challenges one may have in life, challenges that often destroy the gifts and promises into which they were born. Vice

President Burr died in relative obscurity after a duel with Alexander Hamilton, while prescription drug abuse ended the career and the life of Elvis Presley at the young age of forty-two. Both confronted challenges that eventually destroyed their careers.

There have been others born with amazing talents who worked assiduously to overcome those challenges—or at least control them. Diana Ross was born with a beautiful voice but also into abject poverty, and she used one and overcame the other to become, according to *Billboard Magazine*, the greatest female entertainer of the twentieth century. Stephen Hawking was born with a brilliant mind and a horrendous disease, and he used one and overcame the other to become the preeminent physician of his day. Mr. Hawking is now buried among the greatest of Englanders at Westminster Abbey. And Aaron Rodgers was born with amazing quarterback skills but received few offers to play collegiate football, yet he used one and overcame the other to be considered one of the best quarterbacks to ever play the game. We may not have Diana Ross's voice, Stephen Hawking's mind, or Aaron Rodgers's arm, but everyone has something. What you do with that something can make you a somebody—if you choose to do something with it.

In the end, we do not all walk the same road or travel the same path, but we are all given a road to walk and a path to travel. The manner in which we walk along that path determines our success or failure, our greatness or insignificance, and our happiness or heartache. Those who live their own lives, dream their own dreams, develop their own talents, and follow their own ambitions, those who fight the good fight, do the right thing at the right time and for the right reason, and make the most of the roads they travel are the ones that fame and fortune shine the brightest upon. They made the most of what they have, and they did the best with what they had. They did something with their time and talents, and in doing so, they made the world a little bit better. They did not just count the years in a life; they made a difference with the years they were granted. That remains one of the crowning achievements of those who travel this earth.

Have Options in Life

Options give you opportunities,
opportunities give you possibilities,
and possibilities give you hope.

Each century has its trial and tribulations. As we enter the twenty-first century, we encounter a period of profound change, an era of tempestuous anxiety, and an age of prodigious uncertainty. Success seems to be followed by failure far too quickly, and hope seems to be trailed by despair far too closely. Winston Churchill may have been the greatest person who lived in the twentieth century. While serving as prime minister of Great Britain, he helped lead the Allies to victory in World War II. However, shortly after his victory in World War II, he was voted from office by the electorate.

Mr. Churchill is often referred to as England's greatest wartime prime minister. Margaret Thatcher, similarly, has been referred to as England's greatest peacetime prime minister. She was the first woman to serve as prime minister of a Western country and the first to win three elections as prime minister of her country. Then, after almost eleven years in power, her own party removed her from office.

In the United States, Richard Nixon became one of the seminal politicians of his age. He served as a senator and vice president, and in 1968, he was elected president of the United States. At one point, in certain areas, he achieved historic successes as president by opening China to the world and establishing diplomatic relations with the Soviet Union. Mr. Nixon's margin of victory in 1972 has not been equaled in fifty years, and it remains the fourth-highest margin of victory in United States presidential election history. Yet, two years later he was impeached from office.

Churchill, Thatcher, and Nixon all assumed office during turbulent times, confronting events not of their making (World War II, the Vietnam War, socialism in Great Britain), yet they assumed responsibility and resolved them. They all enjoyed spectacular success, yet that success did not translate into future appointment or election. They were removed from office against their will and to the utter disbelief of many. Afterward, each wandered—at times, aimlessly—to find something of value to do after they were removed.

Churchill continued to paint, Nixon turned to writing, and Thatcher traveled widely and gave highly paid speeches. These lessons lead us to an unfortunate truism in life: no matter one's history, no matter one's achievement, no matter one's greatness … nothing lasts. The enormity of one's past triumphs does not immunize one from the shifting winds of the world. And that truism leads to a lesson to be learned: to attain some semblance of security in one's present and balance in one's future, one must have more than one option to pursue and more than one avenue to travel.

There are those who believe they are controlled by factors beyond their control and that the successes and failures they achieve are a consequence of timing and luck. Others work to take charge of those factors within their control, make something of what they have, and do something with what they have been given. The fact is that we have far greater control over how we spend our time on this earth and what we do with the time we have been granted than most believe. We can choose to study or play, work or relax, invest or spend, participate or contribute, and take or give back. The choices we make determine the destiny, and the destiny we pursue determines our legacy.

Those who have the greatest control over their futures are those who have options in life. They do not rely on their current jobs to sustain themselves and their families; they have other prospects to obtain other jobs, or better jobs, should the situation arise. They have invested time and effort into broadening their abilities and capabilities, and as a result, they will never become dependent on one person or one organization to secure their livelihood.

These individuals had options not because they were fortunate— or because luck shined upon their day—but because they worked for it. They worked hard, were unfailingly kind, and overcame any challenges in their paths. They worked to be the type of person who organizations want to work with and employees want to work for. These actions all give a person options in life. Options give you opportunities, opportunities give you possibilities, and possibilities give you hope: the hope that failure will be displaced by success, and bad will be replaced by good.

Options matter—mainly because nothing lasts. In 1500 BC, Egypt was the most powerful country on earth. By 500 BC, Iran had assumed that mantle, with Italy dominant by AD 300 and Spain by

AD 1500. In the past centuries, countries have risen and fallen at a much greater rate and pace. In the 1700s, France controlled much of Europe. By the 1800s, Britain ruled the landscape. In the early 1900s, no country dominated the world like the United States. In fact, the 1900s were the golden age of the United States, represented by advances in medicine, weapons systems, transportation, technology, and computerization unrivaled at any time in history. It is quite possible that no country has been more dominant—economically, socially, culturally, and militarily—than the United States at that point. In the twenty-first century, the United States has been ceding its world dominance to China, which is expected to overtake the United States as the dominant country—at least economically—by 2029, if not sooner.

During the dominating century of the United States, few terms referred to the American philosophy other than the "rugged individual," which typified the American spirit, representative of a person who worked hard, saved their money, had the right idea, and took a chance to invest in their own future. Generations benefited from this spirit, creating new business and new industries, lifting millions into the middle class, and cementing the American dream— which is a rising and improving standard of living from one generation to another—as a reality for those who were willing to work for it. But just as Egypt gave way to Rome and Spain gave way to France, the United States teeters on giving way to another country.

The spectacular technological advances that formed the foundation of the American ascendency to dominance in the twentieth century are the same advances causing its fall: transformational technological advances, such as robotics and artificial intelligence. As we have learned, by 2030 almost 40 percent of jobs in the United States are projected to be eliminated, extinguishing the hopes and dreams of those seeking not just a better life, but a life similar to their parents, both of which appear beyond the reach of our nation's citizens.

In this era of diminishing opportunities, the successful are those who amass the broadest educations, the broadest experiences, and the broadest networks; those who work the most, save the most, and risk the most; and those who have the best skills, make the best choices, and generate the best ideas. More than anything, however, the triumphant are those who have options in life: the option to leave one job for another and to replace one source of income with another. Options give you stability, security, peace, and prosperity—and they give you the possibility of doing something different and being someone different.

Those without options must resign themselves to a future not of their own choosing. They will be dependent on the benevolence of another person or another organization. They will be at the mercy of others, journeying along a path that may not be consistent with their beliefs, ideals, or aspirations. Yet those with options have choices and possibilities, the choice to journey along a different road, and the possibility of something better. In an age where the unfortunate and inevitable often arises, for those with options, the consequences are not catastrophic. They offer an opportunity to do something new, something different, something better.

In some ways, the American dream has not been extinguished. The hopes and dreams of a better life are still alive for those who create options in their lives, bringing a boundless and limitless spectrum of opportunities and possibilities to nearly any path upon which they travel.

> *No matter one's history,*
> *no matter one's achievements,*
> *no matter one's greatness,*
> *nothing lasts.*

Always Look for the Good along the Road of Life

> *No matter who we are or what we do,*
> *who we meet or where we go,*
> *there is good along the roads we travel—*
> *if only we choose to look for it.*

There are those who believe we live in a cold and vindictive world where the ambitions of the one outweighs the interests of the many. They believe there are more lies than truths, more enemies than friends, and more selfishness than generosity. Challenges are seen as more formidable than opportunities, and a sense of defeat pervades one's mind rather than the potential for success.

Conversely, there are those who believe we live in a warm and giving world where individuals contribute their unique talents and spirits to make something or someone better. They believe in the basic decencies and grace of their fellow human beings, and they actively conspire to spread cheer and goodwill through all the corners they travel. Of the two perspectives, which is the more admired of a person and more demanded of an employee? It is the person who chooses, and sees, the good that consumes our present, who believes more in hope than in hopelessness.

Attitudes do matter, and attitudes can determine your fortune. The bright, sunny, and positive dispositions reflective of happy, content, and good people are constructive to a person, which volumes of studies and statistics attest to:

- Happy employees are less likely to get sick, have lower heart rates, have lower levels of stress, and have a 77 percent lower risk of heart disease (Happify.com, 2015, Newman, 2015).
- Positive employees cost employers 41 percent less in health costs (Happify.com, 2015).
- Optimistic people live longer than pessimistic people, an average of 7.5 years longer (Happify.com, Newman 2015).
- Happy people have more friends, and those with more than ten friends live longer (Lyubomirsky, 2008).
- Those with a good attitude and perspective relax more and sleep better (Lyubomirsky, 2008).
- Finally, happy employees and people make more money, mainly because they are more optimistic, have fewer sick days, get better performance reviews, invest in themselves, and are more productive (Lyubomirsky, 2008; Revesencio, 2015; Huddleston, 2017)

You cannot have it all, but you can appreciate what you have. Very little that happened yesterday can be changed today, but you can be grateful for where you have been and what you have done. More importantly, you may not be where you want to be in your life, but you can believe that what comes next will be better than what came before. We live in a world where more good happens than bad, where accomplishments outnumber failures, and where charity outweighs selfishness. Yet far too many focus on failures rather than success, losses rather than victories, trials rather than journeys, tribulations rather than achievements, criticism rather than praise, and envy rather than appreciation. Such are the times in which we live, though it is not the way we should choose to live.

It is unfortunate for those who lead tormented, vindictive, jealous, and even sad lives. While challenges are a surety in life—some determined by fate, others by our own choices—no one goes through this life unscathed. Numerous marriages end in divorce, many lose their jobs, some friends betray trust, and a person's health may become compromised, but for the most part, we choose the manner in which we live: how we work, how we think, how we play, how we behave, and how we treat others. We can choose whether to be happy or sad, helpful or harmful, honorable or shameful, truthful or deceitful, kind or cruel. These are choices that are within our control—if we choose to exercise that control.

No matter the circumstance we encounter, the choices we make, or the roads we take, there is good in life. Nearly everyone we meet can see, hear, smell, and walk; most have food to eat, good health, a safe place to live, a job that affords them a decent standard of living, friends to spend time with, are loved by someone, and have someone to love. These are more than just the basics of life; they are the cornerstones of a good life, and they form the foundation upon which we have pride in our past, happiness in our present, and hope in our future.

Our world may not be easy to live in, but it would be impossible to inhabit this world if we did not look for the good as we travel through its wonders. More than just looking for the good, though, we should be consumed with promoting the good: to say something positive to those who say everything negative about you, to love your friends and not hate your enemies, to applaud the fortunate and help the unfortunate, and to appreciate what you have been given even if it appears less than what others may have been given. It means that no matter the challenge, lie, betrayal, evil, obstacle, jealousy, or treachery you encounter, you search for the good—for the genuine kindnesses and compassions, the goodwill, and the good cheer—that form the foundations of how good people choose to live good lives.

If we can choose to be people of good cheer and good actions, our journeys will be consumed with a sense of honor, decency, and genuine happiness that may be foreign to some and serve as a shining beacon to others of a well-lived life with wondrous possibilities that await those who choose to look for something better, something good, along the roads they travel.

They Have to Live That Life

Those at the other end of the moral spectrum,
who lie, cheat, and steal to advance their selfish interests …
will never find peace, love, and happiness,
and we should let them live that life.

As we traverse through the lands of this earth, we meet those of all backgrounds, cultures, customs, religions, and faiths. We meet the most kind, the most generous, and the most giving people who inhabit the cities and towns we visit. We meet individuals like Wendy Kopp, who in her Princeton thesis created Teach For America, an idea encouraging teachers to serve in challenging schools. That idea has turned into a $300 million foundation that aids the placement and support of teachers in the most challenging urban and rural schools. As of 2018, Teach For America has more than ten thousand recent college graduates and professionals teaching in these schools (Teach for America, 2018). For more than twenty years, Wendy has devoted her time, energy, and money to this foundation, and today, more than thirty-five countries have a Teach For America-related organization. It is an amazing example of what one person can do.

We also meet people like Chance the Rapper, a multiple-Grammy-winning singer who hails from Chicago, one of the most violent cities in the United States. Rather than spend his fortune on fancy houses and cars, Chance used his money to create SocialWorks, a foundation that empowers youth to do something positive with their lives. He also advocates for art in public schools, starting the New Change Arts and Literature Fund to place art in public places. Finally, he visits Chicago libraries each month to encourage children to read. Both Wendy and

Chance are solid role models for those seeking to do something good with what they have.

Sadly, we also meet those at the other end of the moral spectrum, those who are among the most deceitful, the most demented, and the most dishonest in our travels. They are a voiceless, faceless, and nameless cautionary tale for those who want to lead unfulfilled lives of wasted opportunities. They are as unworthy of our praise as our attention, yet far too often, it is these individuals who can impact our careers and our lives the most. A disingenuous comment, a baseless claim, or a deceptive action can be damaging to a person's career. We cannot fathom, or understand, the evil that harbors in others or the sad lives these others have lived (lives created, most often, of their own choosing).

Among the challenges in life is how we react to those who have wronged us, lied about our character, betrayed our trust, maligned our reputations, and been deceitful about their true ambitions. These are truly bad people who have done bad things, and those bad things have often cost us great personal or professional damage. Our first instinct is to respond in kind, to settle any score, to inflict similar harm, all the while believing our actions are just and fair. We have now become the betrayer, the maligner, and the deceiver ... exactly the type of person and performing the exact type of actions we once deemed unjust and unfair. We have become someone else, someone we once despised, loathed, and even hated.

A great person is one who can treat others better than they are treated themselves. It is responding to lies with the truth, to jealousy with understanding, to envy with compassion, to hate with friendship, and to evil with goodness. In a world filled with too much hate, too much envy, too much greed, too much dishonesty, and too much jealously—where some are too demeaning, degrading, and disparaging—doing so may be nearly impossible, but the consequences of not doing so can be catastrophic to living the type of life, and becoming the type of person, that represents the best this life has to offer, which is to live and be a person of genuine honor, decency, and goodness.

In his resignation speech on his last day as the president, Richard Nixon said, "Others may hate you, but they don't win unless you hate them back, and then you destroy yourself." To many observers of a public life, President Nixon led a tormented and sad life. He spent too much time confronting every enemy, battling any battle, and settling every score. He concentrated more on who and what he was against than on who and what he was for. Over time, he destroyed himself, ruining the promise that he could use his position as the president of the United States to do good in this world.

President Nixon's life serves as a sad tale that a person does not become a decent, honorable, and good person by what is done to them; they become a decent, honorable, and good person by who they are, what they do, and how they respond to what is done to them. They become a decent person by treating others better than they have been treated, an honorable person by doing something better than others have done, and a good person by being better than others could possibly be.

It may not be easy, but it is not impossible. In fact, it is possible if we do more for others than they do for us, and if we wish the best for others even if they wish the worst for us. That is a fair and just person, one who lives a decent, honorable, and good life. That life is within the grasp of every person reading this book, or hearing this story, if we only so choose to search for, and work toward, living that type of life and becoming that type of person.

Let others live their own lives—even one of sadness, jealously, envy, and hate—and never let it affect the type of life you want to live. Let your mark be that you thought the best, did the best, and hoped for the best in everything you did and everyone you met, no matter the challenges or unfortunate persons you may have met along that path.

Be Extraordinarily Kind

There is no greater epitaph than this:
"Here lies a kindhearted person with a generous soul
who did something good with their time on earth."

Many are raised by their parents, families, and churches to follow the Golden Rule, which states we should treat others like we would like to be treated. The Golden Rule comes from biblical times, either from "do unto others what you want them to do to you" or "so whatever you wish that others would do to you, do also to them" (Matthew, n.d.). No matter the reference or the translation, the meaning and consequence of following the Golden Rule are similar: treat others as you expect to be treated, and the world will be a better place.

Most resent being lied to, cheated upon, stolen from, and talked about. Few seek to be degraded, demeaned, belittled, and betrayed, yet that conduct has become common to some. The Golden Rule, at least to some, has become tarnished. There are those treated worse than they treat others, a circumstance that tempts even those of the strongest character to reply in kind. But *kind* is the operative word: to not respond in kind but instead to *be* kind.

Some become what they see, and some see a world that is more violent, impersonal, and cruel than at any time in history. We are taught to abandon those stranded on the highway, avoid saying hello to strangers, and bolt our doors both day and night. We are searched before we can enter a movie theater, go through metal detectors before we board a plane, and federal buildings are ringed by cement barriers. More than two million people reside in jail, another five million are on probation or parole, and more than three million work in law enforcement or private security (Wagner and Sawyer, 2018). We live in dangerous and difficult times, becoming a country our ancestors could never have envisioned or imagined.

We also live in a world with almost limitless possibilities, with the power to destroy equal to the power to create. Advances in medicine, from pharmaceuticals to organ transplants, have extended the years in our lives. Innovations in technology, from manufacturing to the internet, have raised our standard of living. And discoveries in telecommunication, from Skype to Facebook, have created communities across the globe. But just as these advances, innovations, and discoveries have reconstructed our present, then can also reimagine our future. We can create a future where hope trumps despair, where courage replaces fear, and where good defeats evil, if we only so choose to take that road, a road that starts with displaying a sense of genuine kindness to those we meet, no matter where our travels take us.

Those possessed of genuine kindness think of others before themselves, give more than they take, help more than they are helped, treat others better than they are treated, and sacrifice for the greater good rather than searching for individual advancement. For those who claim it is a self-centered and self-interested world, for the kindhearted, it remains a selfless and charitable one. The choice one makes between these two extremes determines the type of person one becomes, and it is nearly impossible to become a person of goodwill and good cheer if one chooses the former rather than the latter. Those who choose rightly are an exceptional breed indeed; they are considerate and compassionate, and they display an honest and heartfelt kindness to those they barely know or rarely meet. They are the type of person we want to talk with, the person we want to spend time with, the person we want to work with, the person we want to work for, and the person we strive to become.

Search far and wide, we may be challenged to find many such individuals, but just as advances, innovation, and discoveries have changed the world in one direction, then friendly, considerate, and thoughtful individuals can change the world in another. We can learn to be more appreciative of our health, more thankful of our gifts, more grateful for our good fortune, and more solicitous to those at the other end of the spectrum. We can create a more caring world, where kindness and generosity are the rule and not the exception, and where a giving heart, a thoughtful gesture, and a sunny disposition become the hallmark of a decent and honorable people, a people destined to create a society that will last through the ages.

Go Down Swinging

> *The characteristic that separates the winner from the loser*
> *the consequential from the insignificant,*
> *and the good from the great,*
> *is the determination*
> *to go down swinging for what you stand for.*

One of the great Americans to grace its land was Michael Patrick Murphy. Michael was a lieutenant in the United States Navy, one of the few to serve as a Navy SEAL, which is a Special Operations branch of the navy. The members of the SEAL unit—the term *SEAL* stands for sea, air, and land forces—deliver "highly specialized, intensely challenging warfare capabilities that are beyond the means of standard military forces" and "achieve the impossible through critical thinking, sheer willpower, and absolute dedication to their training, their mission, and their fellow Special Operations team members" (www.navy.com/careers/navy-seal). It is one of the most hallowed groups and organizations in the world.

The United States Navy recruits forty thousand new members a year, with about 50 percent interested in becoming SEALs. However, only about 6 percent of applicants meet the minimum requirements, which require a person be between the ages of seventeen and twenty-eight, have excellent vision and physical abilities, and earn a high score on an aptitude test. Those who meet these stringent requirements then must pass a SEAL training that is referred to as "brutal," where only about one in four who apply eventually become a SEAL, joining the approximately two thousand other SEALs currently on active duty in the US military (White, 2018). The SEALs are the best of the best, the elite of the elite, and Lieutenant Murphy became a perfect embodiment of a SEAL.

Lieutenant Murphy was born in 1976, attended one of the premier universities in the United States, and graduated with dual degrees in political science and psychology (United States Navy Medal of Honor, 2018). He was accepted at some of the most prestigious law schools in the country, but he decided to forsake these opportunities in the hopes of becoming a SEAL and serving his country. He became a SEAL in July 2002.

In 2005, Lieutenant Murphy was serving with a team of SEALS in Afghanistan that was shortly to become infamous throughout the country and later immortalized in the movie *Lone Survivor*. Lieutenant Murphy was the officer in charge of a four-person unit tasked with finding a particularly violent militia commander in the region. Their charge was to find the individual and then radio their location to other units. However, while high in the hills of Afghanistan, Mr. Murphy and his unit were spotted by three sheepherders, including a young teen. Mr. Murphy and his men had a decision to make: kill these individuals, including the young boy, so that they would not relay the SEALs' location to the opposition, or let them return to their village. They decided to let them leave.

The sheepherders returned to their village and informed the opposition of Mr. Murphy and his team's location. A fierce firefight ensued, fought over many hours in the roughest of conditions. During the fight, Lieutenant Murphy risked his life by moving from the protective rocks surrounding the scene of the firefight, eventually settling in the open range so he could better signal the military of their position and request immediate assistance. He was shot multiple times while in the open range, including once in the back, while he radioed navy command with his position and requested immediate help. He was able to successfully radio the message to the base, but it cost Lieutenant Murphy his life. The only one of the four to survive was as Marcus Luttrell, who later wrote the best-selling book *Lone Survivor*.

Lieutenant Murphy was known as "The Protector" in his youth because he stood up for others, and he continued to stand up for the less fortunate, eventually leading him to represent the United States against the malevolent aggressions of some in Afghanistan. His actions resulted in his death, but he stood up for what he believed in, a lasting reminder that right does triumph over wrong, that good does conquer evil. Posthumously, Lieutenant Murphy was awarded the Medal of Honor by President George W. Bush, and his name has graced post offices, parks, and even one of the newest, most technically adept navy warships. He is without a doubt a hero, a good and decent man who found wrong and tried to fix it, who found injustice and tried to correct it.

The characteristic that separates the victor from the loser and the good from the great is the determination to go down swinging for who you are and what you stand for. That characteristic is what separates the life of Lieutenant Michael P. Murphy from so many others. It is the courage and resolve to confront any challenge and overcome any obstacle in your path to greatness. While obstacles and challenges are common to every man or woman, it is the uncommon man who possesses the steely fortitude to go down swinging in the hopes of achieving something better—no matter the chance of success, odds of failure, or hardship or adversity encountered. Against any success, the great never waver, never falter, never give up, and never give in on the path to achieve the improbable or the impossible.

These are the very few who bear each burden, pay any price, ensure every criticism—against seemingly insurmountable odds and undefeatable circumstances—to fight injustice, battle hatred, and confront evil. They avoid one of life's great tragedies—joining the masses in doing nothing—and they do something. The many who do little or nothing live lives of abandoned dreams and lost opportunities. Their accomplishments are overshadowed by disappointments, cowardice is harbored rather than courage displayed, time is wasted and promises remain unfulfilled, and paralyzed minds are paired with traumatized souls. Yet others took a different path. Think of Martin Luther King and civil rights, Susan B. Anthony and the women's right to vote, and Winston Churchill and Nazism. Indeed, the great are a solitary breed, unusually possessed of a determination foreign to most others. They display a steely determination to do what is right no matter the consequences or repercussions.

This capacity and capability to go down swinging in the pursuit of greatness is enjoyed by a solitary few. Most are limited by two fears: the fear of failure and the fear of what others think. Many others are haunted by jealousies, envy, and selfishness, causing them to ridicule honorable efforts and applaud honest failures. That journey usually results in an ordinary person and an unremarkable life. They reside at the negative end of the moral spectrum, which is in stark contrast to the few who have learned that the fear of failure only arises through the pursuit of grand adventures, and that the fear of what others think only arises from those without your best interests at heart, who will never travel the extraordinary journey to do something great that ultimately defines their existence.

The courageous and fearless few never shy from the unpopular, principled stand because the battle is worth the fight. They become seminal figures in the books of history. These brave souls confront the realities of an often-harsh world and try to make it better. They overcome their fear, are courageous in their pursuit, and persevere along the often-torturous journey to do the right thing. They never compromise their values and principles because to not do so would make them cowards and betray the promise of a different life, one better for those who could not, or would not, fight for that promise on their own.

Rise or fall, succeed or fail, win or lose, it is these few who forsake the adversity, criticism, and fear so prevalent in society and ultimately create the world we inhabit. They never abdicate their belief or abandon their hope that if they went down swinging, they could become someone better and create something better. These are the ones who are destined for greatness, and they become consequential in history.

Summary

If you have only one option, you are ruled by the option you have.

Marine John Melia was injured in 1992 during a mission in Somalia that killed four and injured another fourteen. He was one of the fortunate few who survived that harrowing experience, and it left an indelible mark on his life. He always believed that he could have done more to help those returning from the battlefield, and years later, he saw his opportunity. Shortly after September 11, 2001, Mr. Melia and some friends were watching news reports of service members returning from the wars of Afghanistan and Iraq. He thought, *I bet that guy's getting ready to go on the same type of journey that I did for a number of years, struggling to figure out what I was going to do after I was retired from the military* (NonProfitPRO, 2008). Mr. Melia believed it was time to do more, and that belief was to become his life's mission.

Shortly after watching that news report, Mr. Melia and his friends raised some monies and delivered backpacks—filled with underwear, socks, CD players, and T-shirts—to those injured while serving their country. It started with delivering backpacks, and today the organization that he cofounded, the Wounded Warrior Project, offers a "full range of support from the first days after injury to a warrior's transition into civilian life and beyond" (Wounded Warrior Project, Annual Report 2005–06). In 1992, Mr. Melia believed more could be done for returning service members; in 2002, Mr. Melia was determined that more would be done.

Over the next fifteen years, Mr. Melia and his friends created and built the Wounded Warrior Project into the showcase charity and service organization it has become. In 2017, the Wounded Warrior Project served more than 130,000 veterans and their family members, spending more than $160 million on wounded warriors, their families, and their caregivers. More than 1,500 service members or their families sign up with the Wounded Warrior Project every month (General WWP FAQs, 2018). This has become Mr. Melia's mission in life—not because it was profitable, not because it was newsworthy, but simply because it was the right thing to do.

Doing the right thing is often an arduous, painstakingly challenging adventure. It requires a person who does the best with what they have, who searches for options in life, who always looks for the good along the road of life, who is extraordinarily kind and generous, who goes down swinging for what they stand for, and who remembers that only the deceitful and dishonest have to live the lives they have chosen. That is the type of person who organizations want to hire, who employees want to work for, and who people want to be friends with. More importantly, it is the type of person who we aspire to become.

Mr. Melia believed in his mission, and he believed in his cause. More than anything, he did something. We cannot do everything, but we can at least do something. We can build a reputation and establish a legacy of a person who is decent and honorable, who tries to do what is good and what is right, and who is willing to sacrifice all with the hope to make something better. At the end of our days, there are few better stories of a life well lived than that they tried to do something good with what they had, and that they made a difference with their time on this earth.

Rise or fall, succeed or fail, win or lose,
the few who forsake the adversity, the fear, and the criticism that permeates
some in society today create the world in which we live.

The Backpack

True friends don't care who you are.
True friends don't care what you are.
True friends just care.

The search to make a difference—one that defines our existence and determines our legacy—is the seminal journey of life. Those who want to make a difference endure the uncertainties, challenges, and difficulties associated with great change. Through struggles and challenges, the will to make a difference and make something better for others overpowers the will to make something better for ourselves.

A sense of pride and hope pervades those whose interests far exceed their own, and this ambition can be intoxicating for the individual who comes to believe in the power of a different, yet better, future. It is this type of person who seeks to make a difference in the lives of others.

In the dawn of life, we strive to make a living; in the twilight of life, we strive to make a difference. In our younger years, we spent more than we saved, used more than we made, and took more than we gave. Education, experiences, influences, and maturity change our perspectives as time advances. If we realize we made a life, but not a difference, that disappointment and regret will haunt our souls. We strive to make a difference because we realize we have not.

If only we strived to make a difference throughout the entirety of our life rather than only at the end when the sands of time slip through the hourglass. What if we worked to save the environment, shelter the homeless, and feed the hungry in our younger years? What if we helped those with speech impediments speak more fluidly or advised high school seniors how to weather the life-altering experiences as a college freshman? Quite possibly, we could have changed the trajectory of their futures rather than waiting until their fates had been determined.

This reminds me of a story I wrote some time ago: "The Story of the Backpack." I believe that when we are born, we are given a backpack with certain traits, characteristics, talents, and advantages. We spend the remaining moments of our life perfecting those traits, characteristics, talents, and advantages. We spend our lives trying to do something with what we were given in that backpack. It matters little whether we ever achieved our hopes and dreams ... what matters is that we tried. We will never have global peace, feed all the world's hungry, or cure catastrophic diseases and illnesses. What matters is that we tried, that we worked to make the world a better place. What matters is that—at the end of your life—you can return the backpack and say that you did the best you could with what you had, that you fought the good fight, that you did what was right, and that—in some small way—your life made a difference in this world.

It is the reason I carry a backpack every day of my life.

In the end, we are only limited by our dreams of a better world and our determination to make a difference. We can help others be grateful for what they have and not ungrateful for what they do not have, to give more than they take, to assume responsibility for their actions rather than seeking others to blame for their own misdeeds, and rebuild our planet rather than destroying its natural resources. We can help ourselves by always looking for the good along the road of life, go down swinging for what we stand for, and doing something—anything—with our time on earth to contribute to the betterment of humankind. If this can be said as we enter the later stages of our lives, we can say our lives had true meaning, that we mattered, and that, in some small way, we made a difference with our time here on earth.

REFERENCES

Adler, Lou. (2016). New survey reveals 85% of all jobs are filled via networking. LinkedIn.com. February 28, 2016. Retrieved on May 7, 2018, from https://www.linkedin.com/pulse/new-survey-reveals-85-all-jobs-filled-via-networking-lou-adler/

Ag and food sectors of the economy. (2018). United States Department of Agriculture: Economic Research Studies. May 2, 2018. Retrieved on May 7, 2018, from https://www.ers.usda.gov/data-products/ag-and-food-statistics-charting-the-essentials/ag-and-food-sectors-and-the-economy/

Amadeo, Kimberly. (2017). International trade: Pros, cons, effect on economy. *The Balance.* October 6, 2017. Retrieved on February 20, 2018, from https://www.thebalance.com/international-trade-pros-cons-effect-on-economy-3305579

Associated Press. (2016). Robots are taking more factory jobs than Mexico or China. *New York Post.* November 2, 2016. https://nypost.com/2016/11/02/robots-are-taking-more-factory-jobs-than-mexico-or-china/

Biography. (2018). Dr. Seuss Biography. *Biography.* February 6, 2018. Retrieved on July 8, 2018, from https://www.biography.com/people/dr-seuss-9479638

Brushwiz. (2018). Top 100 masterpieces—world's most famous paintings. *Brushwiz.* Retrieved on July 14, 2018, from https://www.brushwiz.com/most-famous-paintings/

Buttonwood. (2018). The manufacturing jobs delusion. *The Economist.* January 4, 2017. Retrieved on February 15,

2018, from https://www.economist.com/buttonwoods-notebook/2017/01/04/the-manufacturing-jobs-delusion

Bureau of Labor Statistics (2018). Economic News Release: Average hourly and weekly earnings of production and nonsupervisory employees on non-farm payroll. Bureau of Labor Statistics. https://www.bls.gov/news.release/empsit.t24.htm

Brown, Meta., & Setren, Elizabeth., & Topa, Giorgio. (2014). Do informal referrals lead to better matches? Evidence from a firm's employee referral system. IZA Discussion Paper No. 8175. May 24, 2014. Available at SSRN: https://ssrn.com/abstract=2441471

Bureau of Labor Statistics, 2015. National Longitudinal Survey: Number of jobs held in a lifetime. Bureau of Labor Statistics. Retrieved on June 10, 2018, from https://www.bls.gov/nls/nlsfaqs.htm

Cakebread, Caroline. (2017). Amazon is now the size of a country. *The Sydney Morning Herald*. October 28, 2017. Retrieved on June 4, 2018, from https://www.smh.com.au/business/companies/amazon-is-now-the-size-of-a-small-country-20171028-gza4cj.html

CareerBuilder. (2015). The Recruitment Power Shift: How candidates are powering the economy. CareerBuilder. Retrieved on June 1, 2018, from http://carluccidesign.com/archive/projects/CareerBuilders/cbParallax4/index.php

CareerBuilder. (2017). Living paycheck to paycheck is a way of life for majority of US. workers. CareerBuilder. August 24, 2017. Retrieved on May 2, 2018, from http://press.careerbuilder.com/2017-08-24-Living-Paycheck-to-Paycheck-is-a-Way-of-Life-for-Majority-of-U-S-Workers-According-to-New-CareerBuilder-Survey

Clairmont, Nicholas. (n.d.). Those who do not learn from history are doomed to repeat it. Really? *Bigthink*. Retrieved on May 1, 2018. https://bigthink.com/the-proverbial-skeptic/those-who-do-not-learn-history-doomed-to-repeat-it-really

Court Statistic Project. (2017). National Overview. Court Statistic Project. Retrieved on April 5, 2018, from http://www.courtstatistics.org/National-Overview.aspx

Crispin, Gerry., and & Mehler, Mark. (2014. Source of Hire Report 2014. *CareerXroads.* September 2014. https://www.careerxroads.com/news/2014_SourceOfHire.pdf

Cummins, Joseph. (2018). During the early 1800s, most Americans earned their living as what? *Sciencing.* Retrieved on February 4, 2018, from https://sciencing.com/during-early-1800s-americans-earned-living-what-12580.html

Doyle, Alison. (2017). How to use networking to find a job. *thebalancecareers.* September 18, 2017. Retrieved on January 4, 2018, from https://www.thebalance.com/how-to-use-networking-to-find-a-job-2058686

Doyle, Alison. 2018. How often do people change jobs? *thebalancecareers.* January 24, 2018. Retrieved on March 5, 2018, from https://www.thebalance.com/how-often-do-people-change-jobs-2060467

Doyle, Alison. April 15, 2018. How long does it take to find a job? *thebalancecareers.* April 15, 2018. Retrieved on May 5, 2018, from https://www.thebalancecareers.com/how-long-does-it-take-to-find-a-job-2064245

Durden, Tyler. December 25, 2016. Top ex-White House economist admits 94% of all new Jobs under Obama were part-time. *ZeroHedge.* Retrieved on May 2, 2018, from https://www.zerohedge.com/news/2016-12-23/top-white-house-economist-admits-94-all-new-jobs-under-obama-were-part-time

Economy, Peter. (2015). 11 interesting hiring statistics you should know. *Inc.com.* May 5, 2015. Retrieved on May 17, 2018, from https://www.inc.com/peter-economy/19-interesting-hiring-statistics-you-should-know.html.

Federal Reserve Bank of St. Louis. (2017). Dissecting the falling labor force participation rate. Federal Reserve Bank of St. Louis. January 3, 2017. https://www.stlouisfed

.org/on-the-economy/2017/january/dissecting-falling-labor-force-participation-rate

Gartenstein, Devra. (2018). Cost of employee benefits for an employer. *The Chron.* March 15, 2018. Retrieved on April 5, 2018, from http://smallbusiness.chron.com/cost-employee-benefits-employer-2694.html

General WWP FAQs. (2018). Wounded Warrior Project. Retrieved on May 21, 2018, from https://www.woundedwarriorproject.org/general-wwp-faqs

Gillett, Rachel. (2016). The story behind Dr. Seuss's first book teaching us something crucial about risk. *Business Insider.* January 17, 2016. Retrieved on June 10, 2018, from http://www.businessinsider.com/the-story-behind-dr-seuss-first-book-teaches-us-something-crucial-about-risk-2016-1

Gittleson, Kim. (2012). Can a company live forever? BBC News. January 18, 2012. Retrieved on April 26, 2018, from http://www.bbc.com/news/business-16611040

Glaser, April., & Molla, Rani. (2017). The number of robots sold in the US will jump nearly 300 percent in nine years. *Recode.* April 3, 2017. Retrieved on May 5, 2018, from https://www.recode.net/2017/4/3/15123006/robots-sold-america-growth-300-percent-jobs-automation.

Halle, Howard. (2018). The best paintings of all time, Ranked. *TimeOut New York.* May 15, 2018. Retrieved on July 7, 2018, from https://www.timeout.com/newyork/art/top-famous-paintings-in-art-history-ranked

Happify.com. (2015). If you're happy and you know it, here's how your health is definitely going to show it. *Prevention.* February 24, 2015. Retrieved from https://www.prevention.com/health/a20445209/happy-people-are-less-likely-to-get-sick/

Harden, Paige. (2016). How to land a job by networking. *Washington Post.* May 23, 2016 Retrieved on May 8, 2018, from https://jobs.washingtonpost.com/article/how-to-land-a-job-by-networking/

Hartmans, Avery. (2017). 15 fascinating facts you probably didn't know about Amazon. *Business Insider.* April 9, 2017. Retrieved on March 5, 2018, from http://www.businessinsider.com/jeff-bezos-amazon-history-facts-2017-4

Hill, Catey. (2017). 10 jobs robots already do better than you. *MarketWatch.* June 30, 2017. Retrieved on March 7, 2018, from https://www.marketwatch.com/story/9-jobs-robots-already-do-better-than-you-2014-01-27.

History. (2018). Common Market Founded. *History.* Retrieved on July 15, 2018, from https://www.history.com/this-day-in-history/common-market-founded

History Lists. (2018). 20 of the world's most famous art pieces. *History.* Retrieved on July 8, 2018, from http://historylists.org/art/20-of-the-world%E2%80%99s-most-famous-art-pieces.html

Huddleston, C. (2017). Why happy people earn more money. *HuffPost.* December 6, 2017. Retrieved from https://www.huffingtonpost.com/gobankingrates/why-happy-people-earn-mor_b_8038640.html

Iyengar, Rishi. (2015). This is how long your business will last, according to science. *Time.com.* Retrieved on April 26, 2018, from http://fortune.com/2015/04/02/this-is-how-long-your-business-will-last-according-to-science/

Kelly, Martin. (2018). Notable American inventors of the Industrial Revolution. *ThoughtCo.* April 22, 2018. Retrieved on May 3, 2018, from https://www.thoughtco.com/top-significant-industrial-revolution-inventors-104725

Long, Heather. (2017). Half the jobs in America pay less than $18 an hour. Can Trump Help? *Washington Post.* August 24, 2017. Retrieved on May 8 from https://www.washingtonpost.com/news/wonk/wp/2017/08/24/half-the-jobs-in-america-pay-under-18-an-hour-can-trump-help/?utm_term=.0d72f6adf078

Lyubomirsky, S. (2008). *The How of Happiness: A New Approach to Getting the Life You Want.* London, United Kingdom: Penguin

Books. Retrieved from on May 15, 2018, from http://greatergood.berkeley.edu/topic/happiness/definition

Lyubomirsky, S., King, L. (2005) The benefits of frequent positive affect: Does happiness lead to success? *Psychological Bulletin.* Volume 131, No. 6. Retrieved on June 2, 2018, from http://www.apa.org/pubs/journals/releases/bul-1316803.pdf

Mallon, Morganne. (2014). Penn State alumnus Michael P. Murphy lives on through family, friends, and *Lone Survivor. Penn State Daily Collegian.* January 27, 2014. Retrieved on May 15, 2018, from http://www.collegian.psu.edu/arts_and_entertainment/article_2044b432-86f3-11e3-8e06-001a4bcf6878.html

Manjoo, Farhad. (2017). How to make America's robots great again. *The New York Times.* January 25, 2017. Accessed on April 4, 2018, from https://www.nytimes.com/2017/01/25/technology/personaltech/how-to-make-americas-robots-great-again.html

Marker, Scott. (2015). How many jobs will the average person have in his or her lifetime? *Linkedin.com.* February 22, 2015. https://www.linkedin.com/pulse/how-many-jobs-average-person-have-his-her-lifetime-scott-marker/

MarketWatch. (2017). The number of reluctant part-time workers is still higher than before the Great Recession. April 9, 2017. Retrieved on February 8, 2018, from https://www.marketwatch.com/story/amazon-will-create-30000-part-time-jobs-but-american-workers-are-desperate-to-work-full-time-2017-04-06

Masunaga, Samantha. Robots (2017). Robots could take over 38% of US jobs within about 15 years, report says. *Los Angeles Times.* March 24, 2017. Retrieved on May 5, 2018, from http://www.latimes.com/business/la-fi-pwc-robotics-jobs-20170324-story.html

Matthew. (n.d.). The Holy Bible, English Standard Version. Retrieved on March 13, 2018, from https://www.biblegateway.com/passage/?search=Matthew+7%3A12&version=ESV

McFarland, Matt. (2017). Robots: Is your job at risk? CNN Tech. September 15, 2017. Accessed on June 1, 2018, from http://money.cnn.com/2017/09/15/technology/jobs-robots/index.html

Mislinski, Jill. (2018). The ratio of part-time employed. *Advisor Perspectives.* February 5, 2018. Accessed on January 5, 2018, from https://www.advisorperspectives.com/dshort/updates/2018/02/05/the-ratio-of-part-time-employed-january-2018

Mutikani, Lucia. (2017). US services sector growth accelerates; trade deficit edges up. *Business News.* September 6, 2017. Retrieved on May 15, 2018, from https://data.worldbank.org/indicator/NV.SRV.TETC.ZS

Sawe, Elisha. (2017). The 10 most famous paintings in the world and where to see them. *World Atlas.* Retrieved on July 8, 2018, from https://www.worldatlas.com/articles/where-to-see-the-10-most-famous-painting-of-the-world.html

United States Navy (n.d.). Medal of Honor, USN Recipients: Lieutenant Michael P. Murphy (SEAL). *United States Navy.* Retrieved on May 10, 2018, from http://www.navy.mil/ah_online/moh/murphy.html

United States Navy (n.d.). Navy Seal Careers. *United States Navy.* Retrieved on May 15, 2018, from https://www.navy.com/careers/navy-seal

The National. (2018). Chinese economic power will dominate the 21st Century. *The National.* October 23, 2017. Retrieved on July 1, 2018, from https://www.thenational.ae/world/asia/chinese-economic-power-will-dominate-the-21st-century-1.669759

Newman, K. M. (2015). 6 scientific facts that link happiness with good health. *Goodnet.* September 2, 2018. Retrieved on February 5, 2018, from https://www.goodnet.org/articles/6-scientific-facts-that-link-happiness-good-health

New York Times. (1988). Farm population lowest since 1850s. *New York Times.* July 20, 1988. Retrieved on May 5, 2018, from https://www.nytimes.com/1988/07/20/us/farm-population-lowest-since-1850-s.html

NonProfitPRO. (2008). Wounded Warrior Project History. *NonProfitPRO.* June 1, 2008. Retrieved on Mary 20, 2018, from https://www.nonprofitpro.com/article/wounded-warrior-project-history-107420/all/

Office of the United States Trade Representative. (2018). North American Free Trade Agreement. *United States Trade Representative.* Retrieved on July 6, 2018, from https://ustr.gov/trade-agreements/free-trade-agreements/north-american-free-trade-agreement-nafta

Pettinger, Tejvan. (2017). Sectors of the Economy. *Economics.* July 19, 2017. Retrieved on April 7, 2018, from https://www.economicshelp.org/blog/12436/concepts/sectors-economy/

Pofeldt, Elaine. (2015). Shocker: 40% of workers now have 'contingent' jobs, says US Government. *Forbes.* May 25, 2015. Retrieved on February 5, 2018, from https://www.forbes.com/forbes/welcome/?toURL=https://www.forbes.com/sites/elainepofeldt/2015/05/25/shocker-40-of-workers-now-have-contingent-jobs-says-u-s-government/&refURL=https://www.google.com/&referrer=https://www.google.com/

Poker Hand Probabilities. (2018). Possible Poker hands in a 52-card deck. *Chemical-ecology.net.* Retrieved on May 8, 2018, from http://www.chemical-ecology.net/java/possible.htm

Rawlinson, Nik. (2017). History of Apple: The story of Steve Jobs and the company he founded. *Macworld.* April 25, 2017. Retrieved on May 2, 2018, from https://www.macworld.co.uk/feature/apple/history-of-apple-steve-jobs-mac-3606104/

Revesencio, Jonha. (2015). Why happy employees are 12% more productive. *Fast Company.* 2015. Retrieved on January 15, 2018, from https://www.fastcompany.com/3048751/happy-employees-are-12-more-productive-at-work

Robotics Industry News. (2016). North American robotics market sets new records in 2015. *Robotics Industry News.* February 10, 2016. https://www.robotics.org/

content-detail.cfm/Industrial-Robotics-News/North-American-Robotics-Market-Sets-New-Records-in-2015/content_id/5951

Ronaldo, Cristiano. (2018). Career Timeline. *Cristiano Ronaldo*. Retrieved on June 30, 2018, from https://www.cristianoronaldo.com/career

Sirkin, Hal., & Zinser, Michael., & Rose, Justin. (2015). The robotics revolution: The next great leap in manufacturing. *BCG.com*. September 23, 2015. Retrieved on June 15, 2018, from https://www.bcg.com/publications/2015/lean-manufacturing-innovation-robotics-revolution-next-great-leap-manufacturing.aspx

Smabaugh, Jay., & Nunn, Ryan., & Liu, Patrick., & Nantz, Greg. (2017). Thirteen Facts about wages growth. *Brookings Institute*. September 25, 2017. Retrieved on January 15, 2018, from https://www.brookings.edu/research/thirteen-facts-about-wage-growth/

Smith, Matthew. (2017). Cristiano Ronaldo opens up about his childhood. *Mail Online*. October 3, 2017. Retrieved on July 3, 2018, from http://www.dailymail.co.uk/sport/football/article-4944376/Real-Madrid-star-Cristiano-Ronaldo-opens-youth.html

Statista. (2018). Distribution of gross domestic product across economic sectors worldwide from 2005 to 2015. *Statista: The Statistics Portal*. Retrieved on May 15, 2018, from https://www.statista.com/statistics/758809/distribution-of-gross-domestic-product-gdp-across-economic-sectors-global/

Statista. (2018). Statistics and Facts about Amazon. *Statista*. Retrieved on June 6, 2018, from https://www.statista.com/topics/846/amazon/

Stettner, Andrew., & Yudken, Joel S., & McCormack, Michael (2017). Why manufacturing jobs are worth saving. *The Century Foundation*. June 13, 2017. Retrieved on January 4, 2018, from https://tcf.org/content/report/manufacturing-jobs-worth-saving/

Sturt, David., & Nordstrom, Todd. (2016). True or false? Employees today only stay one or two years. *Forbes Magazine.* Jan 13, 2016. Retrieved on February 15, 2018, from https://www.forbes.com/sites/davidsturt/2016/01/13/true-or-false-employees-today-only-stay-one-or-two-years/

Sullivan, Emily. (2018). When a full-time job isn't enough to make it. *NPR.* February 2, 2018. Retrieved on June 15, 2018, from https://www.npr.org/2018/02/02/579980199/when-a-full-time-job-isnt-enough-to-make-it

Teach For America. (2018). Wendy Kopp. *Teach For America.* Retrieved on May 15, 2018, from https://www.teachforamerica.org/person/wendy-kopp

UCSF News. (2011). New USCF robotic pharmacy aims to improve patient safety. University of California San Francisco News Center. March 7, 2011. Retrieved on February 2, 2018, from https://www.ucsf.edu/news/2011/03/9510/new-ucsf-robotic-pharmacy-aims-improve-patient-safety

United States Courts. (2018). Federal judicial caseload statistics 2017. United States Courts. Retrieved on February 14, 2018, from http://www.uscourts.gov/statistics-reports/federal-judicial-caseload-statistics-2017

Van Gogh Gallery. (2018). Frequently Asked Questions. Van Gogh Gallery. Retrieved on July 3, 2018, from https://www.vangoghgallery.com/misc/faq.html

Wagner, Peter., & Sawyer, Wendy. (2018). Mass incarceration: The whole pie 2018. *Prison Policy Institute.* Retrieved on June 24, 2018, from https://www.prisonpolicy.org/reports/pie2018.html#dataheader

White, Martha C. (2015). Here's how long it really takes to get a job. *Money.* October 22, 2015. Retrieved on July 5, 2018, from http://time.com/money/4053899/how-long-it-takes-to-get-hired/

White, Ron. (2018). What are the odds of making it into the Navy SEALs. *The Chron.* July 27, 2018. Retrieved on May

15, 2018, from http://work.chron.com/odds-making-navy-seals-26032.html

Williams, Alex. (2017). Will robots take our children's jobs? *The New York Times*. December 11, 2017. Retrieved on January 15, 2018, from https://www.nytimes.com/2017/12/11/style/robots-jobs-children.html

Wilson, Redi. (2014). Watch the US transition from a manufacturing economy to a service economy, in one gif. *The Washington Post*. September 3, 2014. Retrieved on May 2, 2018, from https://www.washingtonpost.com/blogs/govbeat/wp/2014/09/03/watch-the-u-s-transition-from-a-manufacturing-economy-to-a-service-economy-in-one-gif/?noredirect=on&utm_term=.66df364ab35e

Winkel, MC. (2014). Top 20 most expensive paintings in the world. *WHUDAT*. May 25, 2014. Retrieved on June 30, 2019 from https://www.whudat.de/top-20-most-expensive-paintings-in-the-world/

Wiseman, Paul. (2016). Why robots, not trade, are behind so many factory jobs losses. *AP News*. November 2, 2016. Retrieved on May 15, 2018, from https://apnews.com/265cd8fb02fb44a69cf0eaa2063e11d9/mexico-taking-us-factory-jobs-blame-robots-instead

Workopolis. (2016). Why only 2% of applicants actually get interviews. *Careers*. November 10, 2016. Retrieved on June 15, 2018, from https://careers.workopolis.com/advice/only-2-of-applicants-actually-get-interviews-heres-how-to-be-one-of-them/

Wounded Warrior Project Annual Report. (2005–06). Wounded Warrior Project. Retrieved on May 21, 2018, from https://www.woundedwarriorproject.org/media/1051/2005-2006-annual-report.pdf

Zipjob Team. (2017). Why is it so hard to find a job in 2018 and what you should do. *Zipjob*. November 22, 2017. Retrieved on January 15, 2018, from https://www.zipjob.com/blog/why-is-it-so-hard-to-find-a-job/

www.ingramcontent.com/pod-product-compliance
Lightning Source LLC
Chambersburg PA
CBHW030758180526
45163CB00003B/1081